UKRAINIAN LITERATURE IN THE TWENTIETH CENTURY:

A READER'S GUIDE

A nation's literature serves as a mirror of its social and political life. Ukraine, although stateless for most of the twentieth century, is no different in this regard from other lands. Through decades of tremendous political and social changes, Ukrainian literature has reflected the transitions in Ukrainian life.

George S.N. Luckyj provides a survey of the main literary trends of Ukraine, its chief authors, and their works, as seen against the historical background of the present century. He offers his own critical comment and considers as well the opinions of other literary scholars and critics, often in capsule form. Encompassing almost the entire century, the volume shows the growth, the enforced isolation and near-extinction in the 1930s, and, finally, the very lastest revival of Ukrainian literature.

Luckyj provides information about literary developments both in Ukraine and in the Ukrainian emigration and diaspora. The scope of the volume extends to all Ukrainian literature, wherever it was written, and demonstrates how phenomena inside and outside Ukraine emerge as complementary.

The book is published in association with the Shevchenko Scientific Society of New York.

GEORGE S.N. LUCKYJ is Professor Emeritus of Slavic Studies, University of Toronto. He is the author of *Literary Politics in the Soviet Ukraine* and *Between Gogol and Shevchenko*. He is also the editor of *Shevchenko and the Critics,* and translator and editor of Pavlo Zaitsev's *Taras Shevchenko: A Life.*

UKRAINIAN LITERATURE IN THE TWENTIETH CENTURY

A Reader's Guide

GEORGE S.N. LUCKYJ

Published for the Shevchenko Scientific Society by

UNIVERSITY OF TORONTO PRESS

Toronto Buffalo London

© University of Toronto Press 1992
Toronto Buffalo London
Printed in Canada
Reprinted in 2018
ISBN 0-8020-5019-0 (cloth)
ISBN 978-0-8020-6003-7 (paper)

Printed on acid-free paper

Canadian Cataloguing in Publication Data

Luckyj, George, 1919–
  Ukrainian literature in the twentieth century

  Includes index.
  ISBN 0-8020-5019-0 (bound) ISBN 978-0-8020-6003-7 (paper)

  1. Ukrainian literature – 20th century – History
and criticism. 2. Politics and literature –
Ukraine – History – 20th century. 3. Ukraine –
Politics and government – 1917–   . I. Naukove
tovarystvo imeny Shevchenka. II. Title.

  PG3916.2.L83 1992   891.7'909'003   C91-095667-7

Contents

Preface

This brief study is not a literary history. I had neither the time nor the energy to undertake such a major project. It is an attempt to survey the main literary trends, the chief authors, and their works, as seen against the historical background of the present century. The main objective is to provide a pocket-size reader's guide that may be useful to students and to the general public. It does not attempt to provide a complete bibliography, or even to list all the major works. It does, however, offer some critical comment and the opinions of other literary scholars and critics, often in capsule form. My aim is to encompass almost the entire century and to show the growth, the enforced isolation and near-extinction in the 1930s, and, finally, the very latest revival of Ukrainian literature.

There are some areas and periods that are only briefly mentioned, in particular, the era of 'socialist realism.' The plethora of Soviet literary works from that period simply does not belong in any serious literary study, but lies in the sphere of graphomania and yellow (or, perhaps, red) journalism. As such it deserves a separate sociological rather than literary study, but it has contributed little to the general literary achievement. The average Ukrainian reader, by and large, ignored the works that were produced in response to Party demands. Such readers have either returned to the classics, turned to foreign literature, or turned their backs on current Ukrainian literature altogether. The partial abandonment by Ukrainians of their own language may also have been partly caused by the unreadability of Soviet literature.

The reader may find some quotations from the Soviet critics both tedious and tiresome, especially the official criticism of 'socialist realism.' These have been inserted deliberately to give the flavour of the times. It is essential to have some acquaintance with the recorded history of what may now seem faintly ridiculous pronouncements. For decades this was the voice that Soviet Ukrainian writers and their readers heard most frequently.

The present volume takes its bearings from Ukraine's condition as a stateless and oppressed country. It encompasses the moments of national upsurge in 1917–20 and again in 1989–90, as well as the traumatic experiences of the 1930s. Both these ups and downs in the political and social life of the country had an extraordinary impact on literature. Another purpose of this study is to provide information not only about literary developments in Ukraine but also in the Ukrainian emigration and diaspora. The volume includes all Ukrainian literature, wherever it was written. It helps, therefore, to have a broad perspective. Many phenomena, inside and outside Ukraine, emerge as complementary.

The approach taken in the guide is traditional, even old-fashioned. No attention has been paid to current literary critical theory or to new ways of looking at literary history. Some monographs and articles in this area exist and may be consulted by the interested reader. Here, however, such a reader will find only facts, names, titles, and dates, sprinkled with some critical comment and some historical allusions and observations. A panorama will unfold in which the reader will be able to survey the vital developments of Ukrainian literature in this century and to attach critical judgments to them. This concise treatment may stimulate further enquiry into details and encourage the search for a wider knowledge. A reader's guide is but a key to further study. A perceptive user of this key can unlock many closed doors leading to unexplored areas.

I wish to express my thanks to the following colleagues for their help and advice: Bohdan Boychuk, Bohdan Budurowycz, Lidia Palij, Roman Senkus, and Taras Zakydalsky. None bears responsibility for the views and attitudes expressed in this book. Special thanks are due to R. Schoeffel, senior house editor at the University of Toronto Press, and to Darlene Money for her expert copy editing. My greatest debt is to my wife, Moira.

UKRAINIAN LITERATURE IN THE TWENTIETH CENTURY

1 Beginning a New Century

Modernism

To start with modernism is by no means an attempt to ignore the ever-present populism and realism that still ruled supreme at the turn of the nineteenth and twentieth centuries. Ever since the early nineteenth century Ukrainian literature was an expression of national identity. The awakening national consciousness, which first flared up in the romantic poetry of Taras Shevchenko (1814–61), reached a widening readership despite the tsarist bans on Ukrainian publications in 1863, 1876, and 1881. This was made possible by printing works in Ukrainian in Austro-Hungary (Galicia), from where they spread to all of Ukraine. The guiding ideas of this literature were strongly populist and the style was realistic. The life of the downtrodden peasantry was the predominant subject-matter. Yet at the end of the nineteenth century new trends appeared in Ukrainian literature that conveniently go by the name of modernism.

In one of his essays,[1] Ivan Franko, the leading Galician writer and critic, provided an incisive look at the literature of that time. Despite censorship and political oppression Franko saw much progress in Ukrainian literature during the last decades of the nineteenth century. This he attributed to the appearance of some young writers – for example, Krymsky, Khotkevych, Stefanyk, Kotsiubynsky, and Kobylianska – who showed 'a close observation of life, a very serious understanding of art and its social function and strong faith in the future of our national development.'[2] 'Modern versification,' he continued, 'has made great progress towards purity of language and melodiousness in poetry ... our prose ... has acquired poetic flight, melodiousness, grace, and variety ...'3 The young writers had been educated on the best European models, which followed 'the new studies in psychology' and depicted 'inner spiritual conflicts' rather than external events.

This essay was first published in 1901, but three years earlier Franko had written an article 'Internationalism and Nationalism in Modern Literature,'4 in which he characterized, on the whole favourably, the modernist trends in Western European literature, as long as they contained a 'healthy kernel (zdorove zerno).' (Verlaine might be a genius, but was an alcoholic, and Maupassant's obsession with sex was wrong.) Curiously enough, Franko seemed oblivious of fin-de-siècle Vienna, but argued that 'nationalism and internationalism are not at all contradictory.'5 Also in 1898 he published a major essay on aesthetics6 in which he pleaded for literary criticism devoid of political, social, or religious ideas.7 He disagreed with much of the French and German contemporary criticism as well as with the Russian critic Dobroliubov, and pleaded for recognition of the role of the subconscious in literary creation. 'To compare poetic imagination with dreams and, beyond that, with hallucinations is not an idle game.'8 Large parts of the essay were devoted to 'poetry and music' and 'poetry and painting.'

Franko also played a key role in the only literary monthly, *Literaturno-naukovy vistnyk* (Literary and Scientific Herald), which, under the editorship of Mykhailo Hrushevsky, began to appear in Lviv in 1897. Franko was de facto its literary editor and a frequent contributor. Volodymyr Hnatiuk was a third member of the editorial board. The journal stood above the political parties of the time and was truly representative of both Western and Eastern Ukraine. Beginning with its earliest issues the journal devoted much space to Western European literature. Translations and review articles appeared on Maupassant, Verlaine, Kipling, D'Annunzio, Maeterlinck, Ibsen, Strindberg, Hauptmann, Schnitzler, and others. Ukrainian modernist writers such as Vynnychenko, Kobylianska, Iatskiv, Stefanyk, and Oles appeared side by side with such older authors as Nechui-Levytsky and Hrinchenko. In 1907, following the revolution of 1905 and the relaxation of censorship in Russia, the journal was transferred to Kiev.

One issue of the *Herald* in 1901 carried an announcement by Mykola Vorony:

With the aim of compiling and publishing here, in the Black Sea region, the Katerynodar, a Ruthenian-Ukrainian almanac that, in form and content, could at least in part approach the modern currents and trends of contemporary European literature, and wishing to enrol the widest possible range of contributors, I am asking my friends a great favour – kindly to take part in a joint enterprise and with their pens assist in achieving this goal ... Putting aside many worn-out tendencies and compelling morals that again and again have forced our young writers onto the path of cliché and narrow-mindedness and also avoiding works that are blatantly naturalistic and brutal, one would like instead to have works with a small dose of originality, with a free, independent outlook, and with contemporary content. One would like to have works with some philosophy, in which there would shine even a small piece of that distant blue sky, which for centuries has beckoned to us with its unreachable beauty, with its unfathomable mystery ... The closest attention should be paid to the aesthetic aspect of the works.[9]

This modernist appeal materialized two years later with the publication of the almanac Z nad khmar i z dolyn (From above the Clouds and from the Valleys, 1903), edited by Vorony. It was not as radical as its editor would have liked, but it was nevertheless a landmark in Ukrainian literature. Its introduction consisted of a literary duel between Franko and Vorony. Despite a theoretical attack on modernism, Franko contributed to the almanac his fine lyrical poems 'Ziviale lystia' (Withered Leaves). Most contributors – Vorony, Shchurat, Lesia Ukrainka, Karmansky, Kobylianska, Khotkevych, Lypa, Kotsiubynsky, Krymsky – were modernist, but there was also traditional verse and prose by Franko, Hrabovsky, Hrinchenko, Nechui-Levytsky, and Samiilenko. What Vorony had promised was carried out by and large.

There was also, however, considerable opposition to the budding modernism. The major populist critic, Serhii Iefremov, vehemently attacked it in a long series of articles, 'V poiskakh novoi krasoty' (In Search of New Beauty), published in 1902 in Kievskaia starina (Kievan Antiquity). He savaged the feeble 'Poeziia v prozi' (Poetry in Prose) by Hnat Khotkevych and spent most of his anger on Olha Kobylianska. He admitted that she had talent, but was unable to find anything valuable in her short modernist stories or her ambitious feminist novel, Tsarivna (The Princess). The heroine, he argued, was passive, her actions were inadequately motivated, and the idea, borrowed from

Nietzsche, of a striving to be a 'superman' in defiance of the dark mob, unacceptable. Kobylianska's 'aristocratism' was simply based on a 'dubious morality.' She idealized nature and her language was impure. Even her other novel about the peasantry, *Zemlia* (Earth), has serious shortcomings. In the end Iefremov condemned Kobylianska for 'her contempt for simple folk.' Another woman writer, Natalia Kobrynska, drew Iefremov's ire for departing from her early realistic stories and attempting to write like a symbolist. Finally, Iefremov dug up a little-known modernist publisher, *Zhyvi struny* (Living Strings), which published Stanislaw Przybyszewski in Ukrainian. This led him to conclude that the basic tendency of Ukrainian modernism was to glorify sex, a charge that was patently absurd. His fear that in pursuit of 'pure beauty' they had reached 'animal depravity' was quite unjustified. Iefremov's hostility was rooted in his inability to see modernism as a reaction against the status quo. True, many of the modernist products were artistically deficient, yet they could not be regarded, as Iefremov described them, as 'hashish' or as an escape from the writer's real duty to his people.

Unfortunately, the strong reaction to Iefremov's article remained unpublicized. Long letters to *Kievskaia starina* from Lesia Ukrainka and Hnat Khotkevych were not published. Khotkevych also wrote an irate letter to the *Herald*[10] and Lesia Ukrainka expressed her views in private letters.[11] Writing to her mother in 1909, she complained that Iefremov's article was 'a pit into which everything was thrown,' whether a 'decadent' hair-style or 'trendy colours.'[12] Earlier, in a letter to Pavlyk in 1903, she characterized Iefremov's article as 'superficial' and 'blindly certain about areas of which he was ignorant (French literature and the history of modern trends).'[13]

Two years later, in 1904, Iefremov repeated his argument in an article in *Kievskaia starina*, 'Na mertvoi tochke' (At a Standstill), in which he criticized Vorony's almanac very harshly. He also attacked Katria Hrynevycheva's article in the *Herald*,[14] in which she argued that 'no one can criticize what he does not understand.' Iefremov ridiculed Vorony's polemics with Franko and reviewed individual contributions to the almanac with a great deal of sarcasm. They were full of 'vague symbolism,' 'impenetrable mysticism,' 'slavishly imitate foreign models,' 'have nothing positive in them,' and 'are indifferent to social problems.' All this may have been true, yet it did not amount to a serious criticism of the new trend. Iefremov tried to see in modernism only a temporary, transitional phase to a more 'healthy' literature that would serve the interests of the people. In the end he saw such 'fresh strength,' strangely enough, in Vynnychenko's works, and advised Vorony to abandon the 'clouds' and dwell in 'the valleys.'

About the same time, in the first decade of the new century, modernist tendencies in literature appeared in Western Ukraine, which was then under Austrian rule. A loosely organized group of young writers, Moloda Muza (the Young Muse) emerged in 1906. Among its members were Volodymyr Birchak, Stepan Charnetsky, Mykhailo Iatskiv, Petro Karmansky, Ostap Lutsky, Vasyl Pachovsky, Osyp Turiansky, and Sydir Tverdokhlib. Also associated with them was the poet Bohdan Lepky. The composer S. Liudkevych and the sculptor M. Parashchuk were also members of the group. In 1907 Ostap Lutsky published an article in *Dilo* (Deed)[15] that was greeted as a manifesto of the Young Muse. He began by describing the 'new wave' in Western European letters and art that was influenced by the writings of Nietzsche, Ibsen, and Maeterlinck. This 'loss of all hope,' the upheaval in values, and the 'new mystical skies' could also be seen in Ukrainian literature, primarily in the works of Olha Kobylianska. The older writers (Karpenko-Kary, Nechui-Levytsky, Franko, Myrny) held that truth must be 'sensible, objective, and useful to everyone.' The older critics, such as Iefremov, ridiculed those who wrote differently. Yet 'a reaction set in' against the old school in literature. 'Artistic creation,' according to the new school, 'was neither a nurse nor a propagandist'; its only sanction is the 'inner, spiritual need of the creator, which may not be locked into a rational drawer.' Instead of 'cold reason' the new writers follow 'the fires of their own hearts ... Poetry must, above all, be poetry.' This new tendency in literature 'gave us Kobylianska, Stefanyk, Kotsiubynsky, Lesia Ukrainka, Lepky, Shchurat, and many others.'[16] Hence also arose the Young Muse, whose task was to foster the new literature through its publications.

In comparison with Russian and Polish modernist manifestos Lutsky's article was mild and moderate. It simply stated the present literary situation. However, less than a month later, also in *Dilo*,[17] it was viciously attacked by Ivan Franko. At the beginning of his angry reply, which was no doubt also motivated by anger at Lutsky's parodies of his work, Franko reminded his readers that he had in the past favourably reviewed the modernist poetry of Vasyl Pachovsky. He then launched his attack. Franko had never heard that 'God was dead.' Nietzsche's influence was ephemeral and the 'great spiritual crisis' in Europe of which Lutsky was writing was non-existent. He ridiculed the idea that literature must show a new sensibility. In Ukrainian literature Kobylianska's talent 'has recently shown a marked weakening.' Older writers deserved respect, while the new writers had failed to captivate readers with their 'subtleties' and 'sincerity in human relationships.' The latter, wrote Franko, 'must not become part of a "literary program." '[18] At the end he fulminated against the publishing activities of the Young Muse. About the same time there appeared an equally sarcastic review by Franko in the *Herald* of some verse published by the Young Muse.[19] Altogether his attitude to the Young Muse was uncompromising. 'One must put an end,' he wrote in a letter to Hrushevsky, 'to the demoralization, the stupidity, and the pretensions of our Young Muse.'[20]

The harshness of Franko's criticism evoked little protest. His authority remained unchallenged and no real polemic between the traditionalists and the modernists in Ukraine ever took place. It is noteworthy, however, that the defenders of the status quo (Iefremov, Franko) showed occasional appreciation of modernist literature.

For some time – since February, 1906 – the Young Muse had a journal, *Svit* (The World), published by Viacheslav Budzynovsky, but edited by the 'Young Musians.' After the relaxation of censorship following the 1905 revolution in Russia, another modernist journal, in Eastern Ukraine, was established in 1909 in Kiev. It was called, rather traditionally, *Ukrainska khata* (Ukrainian Home). It was edited by Pavlo Bohatsky and Mykyta Shapoval, whose literary pseudonym was Sribliansky. Its leading critic and theoretician was Mykola Ievshan (Fediushka), whose series of essays was published separately.[21] Following Nietzsche and Ruskin Ievshan pleaded for a new aesthetic culture, whose aim would be 'an original and harmonious human being, who would not conflict with others or with himself and who could be self-sufficient and happy.'[22] And again, the role of art, like that of religion, was 'to prepare an elevated atmosphere in the upbringing of individuals and whole generations so that their hearts might accept everything beautiful, joyful, and noble.'[23] Ievshan was a harsh critic of modernist

poetry, calling it 'powerless,' 'without ideas,' and 'isolated from life.'
He liked grandiloquent terminology, calling on his countrymen to
'breathe with full lungs' and to emulate a 'free man.' According to
Sribliansky, impressionism in art and individualism in life were the
ways to 'liberate mankind from all the negative aspects of social life.'[24]

Khatiane (Homers), as they were called, had a large following, not
so much because of the modernist platform, but because, as their editorial policy stated: 'the aim was to turn our thoughts to the path of
progress, where better ideals of humanity are shining – freedom, equal-
ity, brotherhood.'[25] Both Ievshan and Sribliansky were also fervent
nationalists. Among the contributors to the journal were the poets Oles,
Chuprynka, Lepky, Vorony, Cherniavsky, Rylsky, Tychyna and Svidzinsky and the prose writers Vynnychenko, Zhurba, Kobylianska, and
Kybalchych. Among the journalism it produced, by Andrii Tovka-
chevsky and Sribliansky, were articles on American democracy. The
journal, which was often attacked by the newspaper *Rada* (Council), continued till the outbreak of the First World War, when all Ukrainian publications were banned.

On the whole, Ukrainian modernism was moderate, unwilling or
unable to put forward bold new theories, experiment with new styles
and structures, or reach the extreme of 'decadence.' In the best available
treatment of what its author calls Ukrainian 'pre-symbolism,'[26] too
much stress is laid on the innovative achievement of modernism. In
fact, many modernists could not entirely divorce themselves from the
realistic tradition. While preaching 'art for art's sake,' they still wished
to serve the national cause. Their aim was perhaps best expressed in
a letter to Panas Myrny, written in 1903 by Mykhailo Kotsiubynsky
and Mykola Cherniavsky:

For one hundred years of its existence our modern literature (for historical
reasons) was nourished largely by the village, village life, and ethnography.
The peasant, the circumstances of his life, his uncomplicated, for the most part,
psychology – that is almost all that engaged the imagination and talent of the
Ukrainian writer. There are a few exceptions. Our educated reader, brought
up on the better models of contemporary European literature, which is rich
not only in themes but in the manner of constructing plots, has the right to
expect from his native literature a wider field of observation, a true depiction

of all the aspects of life of everybody, not merely one social stratum, and would wish to encounter in our belles-lettres the treatment of philosophical, social, psychological, historical, and other themes.[27]

There was, therefore, a basic agreement on the need for departure from the old themes and modes of expression, but there was less certainty as to where to turn next. The search for new forms lasted for several decades and produced some excellent results. It was, moreover, buoyed up by the revolution of 1917–20 and continued to influence literature till the onset of Stalinism in 1930. It showed the decided impact of Western European literary models and continued Europeanization of Ukrainian literature.

The twentieth century was greeted in the collection of 'exotic' poems by the promising young Oriental scholar, Ahatanhel Krymsky (1871–1942) entitled *Palmove hillia* (Palm Branches, 1901). In his introduction, discussing 'profane' love, he admitted that his works were meant 'not for people who are physically healthy, but for those who are a little sick, with frayed nerves and lacking vigour.'[28] In the poems themselves he confessed his 'subjectivism' and 'egotism,' searching always for 'refined aesthetic feelings.' The 'groans of millions steeped in famine and injustice' did not interest him. The lyrical narrator of *Palm Branches* is similar to Andrii Lahovsky, the hero of his modernistic novel of the same title. Written between 1894 and 1904 this novel, autobiographical despite the author's protestations to the contrary, has all the ingredients of 'decadence': narcissism, sex, homoeroticism, mysticism, even Sufism. In 1905 Lesia Ukrainka wrote a very long letter to Krymsky with the sharp and detailed criticism of a sympathetic reader.[29]

Krymsky was also the author of *Povistky ta eskizy z ukrainskoho zhyttia* (Tales and Sketches from Ukrainian Life, 1896) and *Beirutski opovidannia* (Beirut Short Stories, 1906). Soon after the revolution of 1905 he stopped writing and dedicated himself with great success to scholarship. He was a victim of Stalin's purges in the 1930s, but has been posthumously rehabilitated. Here is a Soviet critic's assessment of his early poetry:

His poetry had everything: juvenile emulation, youthful extremism in the search for truth, and unearthly honesty about himself and others. His hero could be light-hearted and waver and retreat from his own happiness, could quit in the face of love and invent some social reasons for quitting and fleeing far away. He could be pensive, could affirm life and sometimes look at it from the distance of centuries, in order to say that everything is vanity and at the same time conclude that life is worthwhile.

That was Krymsky's poetry, consonant with his time and at the same time unique. Not only because Krymsky's poetic hero was chiefly placed against a background of Syrian and Lebanese landscapes, but because of its merciless truthfulness, which frightened some away and consoled others by being clear and comprehensible. His hero was the product of his era, who condensed within himself the pains and vacillations within someone in a bourgeois society, someone who was talented and exceptional and who thought and sensed everything more subtly and therefore more painfully. This was painful for the Ukrainian intelligentsia who, in addition to the general nervousness of those who were searching for and often could not find a place in this era of imperialism and proletarian revolution, felt very painfully the national oppression of their own freedom-loving and unhappy people.[30]

Another modernist, Vasyl Pachovsky (1878–1942) made his debut in 1901 with a collection of lyrical love poems, *Rozsypani perly* (Scattered Pearls), which was warmly greeted by Franko. Two years later Pachovsky published *Son ukrainskoi nochi* (The Dream of a Ukrainian Night, 1903), a nationalistic poem that foreshadowed his later play, *Sontse ruiny* (The Sun of the Ruin, 1909), which was lacking in real poetic power. However, only in his collection *Ladi i Mareni* (For Lada and Marena, 1912) did he recapture his earlier fire.

Critics have pointed out an affinity between the early Pachovsky and Tychyna.[31] Franko's critique is still the best appraisal of Pachovsky:

Mr Pachovsky has demonstrated to us that he is a great master of our language, a true and talented poet, who has deeply attuned his ear to the melody of our folk-songs and folk language and who has mastered the technique of verse as few among us have; he can, with one touch, move responsive chords in our souls, awakening the desired mood and sustaining it until the end. In a word, in quality and poetic power Mr Pachovsky's book has roused in me enormous, pleasurable surprise ... His poetry flows naturally, unforced, as the simplest expression of his feeling, Even if this feeling is still not very deep and the circle of impressions not wide, even if his melodies are monotonous, all the more credit should be given to his talent, which can express the simplest and most trivial things poetically, not stereotypically, can paint with fresh, not borrowed colours.[32]

Some notoriety was acquired among the modernists by Petro Karmansky (1878–1956), whose collection of poems *Z teky samovbyvtsi* (From the File of a Suicide) was published in 1899. His second collection, *Oi, liuli smutku* (Sleep Well, My Sorrow, 1906), had this characteristic foreword by a friend, Mykhailo Iatskiv: 'We were born by chance, unfortunately, to destroy cheap minds, to disturb the sweet languor of the philistines. We baptize our children with the tears of our people, temper them in the fire of our hearts, and lead them forth to the Temple of Beauty. Here there is some comedy: many do not take us seriously, but our audience is large. This is the lineage of comrade Petro. His book is meant for those who will accompany us, for those, as Przybyszewski wrote, who "hew new paths in the primeval forests" '[33]

Karmansky published other collections of pessimistic lyrics: *Plyvem po moriu tmy* (We Sail on the Sea of Darkness, 1909) and *Al fresco* (1917). He also translated Dante. After the revolution of 1917 he spent some time in South America, producing a travel book, *Mizh ridnymy v pivdennii Amerytsi* (Among Relatives in South America, n.d.). He also left some vivid recollections of the Young Muse – *Ukrainska bohema* (Ukrainian Bohemians, 1936). After 1941 he wrote several pro-Soviet tracts.

Two minor poets of the Young Muse deserve to be mentioned: Stepan Charnetsky (1881–1944) was also a drama critic and a feuilletonist under the pseudonym Tyberii Horobets. He published a collection of poetry, *V hodyny sumerku* (During Twilight Hours, 1908), and some short stories and sketches in *Dyky vynohrad* (Wild Grapes, 1921). Another poet and translator was Sydir Tverdokhlib (1886–1922), author of a collection of verse, *V svichadi plesa* (In the Mirror of the River, 1908). He also wrote short stories and translated from and into Polish – *Antologia współczesnych poetów ukraińskich* (An Anthology of Contemporary Ukrainian Poets, 1911). He was killed by Ukrainian nationalists for his pro-Polish stand.

Bohdan Lepky (1872–1941), who lived in Krakow, where he later taught Ukrainian literature at the university, was a mentor for many younger Galician poets. He was very prolific, publishing many collections of poems, among them *Strichky* (Stanzas, 1902), *Lystky padut* (The Leaves Are Falling, 1902), and *Nad rikoiu* (On the River, 1905), as well as short stories, *Z sela* (From the Village, 1898); a novel, *Pid tykhy vechir* (On a Quiet Evening, 1923); and a tetralogy, *Mazepa* (1926–7). An early Soviet Ukrainian literary scholar summed up Lepky's contribution as follows:

[His] first collections are still strongly influenced by populist lyricism, containing some paraphrases of Shevchenko's poetics. Later Lepky masters the symbolist creative method, taking over to a large extent the urban ideology of modernism with its carnivals, coffee-house, balls, and the morals and mores of the urban bourgeoisie. In this connection the dull, aimless ennui and disillusionment of man, unaccustomed to a new life-style, which dominate in the first collections, are replaced by a more cheerful, combative tone (particularly in the collection *Poezie, rozrado odynoka*, 1908) directed against the apathetic Galician bourgeoisie. On the whole, in Lepky's poetry meditation prevails over direct emotional and imagistic elements ...[34]

Two of the major poets in Eastern Ukraine were modernists: Mykola Vorony and Oleksander Oles. Vorony (1871–1942) received his higher education in the West (Vienna, Lviv) and was first attracted to the theatre and journalism. In 1900, upon returning to Russian Ukraine, he joined the Revolutionary Ukrainian Party (RUP). He published an almanac *Z nad khmar i z dolyn* (see page 5), and continued working for the theatre. His first collections of poems were *Lirychni poezii* (Lyrical Poems, 1912) and *U siaivi mrii* (The Splendour of Dreams, 1913). In the foreword to the latter Spyrydon Cherkasenko wrote: 'The characteristic features of Vorony's creativity are activism, fervour, and search. Organically, he cannot accept old forms and dull repetitions and sees the creation of new forms, new rhythms, images, and symbols as the main task of poetry ... Also there is nothing more sacred for him than Ukraine ... Yet, most of all, Vorony is a poet of love. Woman, this mysterious sphinx, with a smile of heaven and hell, always attracts the poet's attention, his songs of happiness and suffering, his bright faith and deep despair.[35]

A Soviet scholar assessed Vorony's contribution in these words:

The literary predispositions of his poetic work are clear: first of all, a striving to escape from the populist stereotype and, second, to raise Ukrainian poetry to the level of contemporary European poetry. Third, to put forward in theory and practice the principle of pure art, with an absolute renunciation of any tendentiousness ... A thought arises about Vorony's dependence on foreign models. The poet himself pointed out the French poets from whom he learned the craft of verse – especially Verlaine and, in part, Mallarmé. He feels an inner affinity with Verlaine ...[36]

After the failure of the Ukrainian national revolution Vorony left Ukraine for the West. He returned to Ukraine in 1926, however, and saw a volume of his poems published in 1929. During the 1930s he fell victim to the Stalinist purges. He has been rehabilitated and republished posthumously.

Oleksander Oles (real name Kandyba, 1878–1944) was a prolific lyric poet who gained popularity with his collection *Z zhurboiu radist obnialas* (Joy and Sorrow Embraced, 1907), which also greeted the 1905 revolution. He was the author of 'dramatic études': *Po dorozi v kazku* (On the Way to a Fable, 1910) and *Nad Dniprom* (On the Dnieper, 1911). He forecast the tragic failure of the 1917 revolution, after which he emigrated. He lived in Prague from 1924 until his death, continuing to write poems full of nostalgia, despondency, and satire. His 'neo-romanticism' has been criticized by Fylypovych[37] and Zerov:

Oles's poetic manner has been regarded as belonging to symbolist tradition. Fylypovych's article demonstrated the poet's distance from ... symbolism; his feeling for the world consists in a naive contrast between life and a dream, prose and poetry. 'Everything that happens in our life is commonplace' – it is prose. 'Poetry is conceived in nature, untouched by human hand,' 'in the moonlight and amid the stars, in the shadows and mysteries of night with its nightingale, in the spring, which calls to life flowers and butterflies.' This is an imitation of the old romanticism, which survived in Ukrainian and Russian poetry for a long time, declining all the time. For a while, Oles with his direct, strong talent revived it and 'the fire that slept in the ashes' flared up, but only for a short time, to be extinguished forever. Even Oles's symbols have nothing in common with the enveloping of the subject in a complex and whimsical mass of associations, so characteristic of the poetry of Mallarmé, Viacheslav Ivanov, Innokenty Annensky, Blok, etc.[38]

Banned for decades in Soviet Ukraine, Oles's selected poems were republished there in 1964 with a preface by Maksym Rylsky.

Two minor poets with decidedly modernist leanings deserve to be mentioned: Mykola Filiansky (1873–?) and Hrytsko Chuprynka (1879–1921). Filiansky was the author of *Liryka* (Lyrics, 1906), *Calendarium* (1911), and *Tsiluiu zemliu* (I Kiss the Earth, 1928). Ievshan praised *Calendarium* for 'its purity and nobility of tone and its depth ... he succeeded in harmonizing his Ukrainian psyche with elements of modern European, primarily French, poetry.'[39] Chuprynka, who began and ended as a traditionalist, showed some originality in *Ohnetsvit* (Fiery Flower, 1910), which was reviewed by Shapoval as 'gay and light-hearted ... the work of a symbolist poet, and adherent of [pure] art.'[40] Filiansky was arrested in 1937 and perished in the Gulag. Chuprynka was shot by the Bolsheviks in 1921. In 1988 he was rehabilitated, with the following commentary:

Hrytsko Chuprynka's poetry is a *sui generis* cardiogram of the heartbeat of the Ukrainian intelligentsia of the first decade of the twentieth century. This was a complex period of our intellectual history, tied emotionally to an active awakening of the national consciousness and the inevitable new paths of cultural and literary development, a dynamic pursuit of new images, forms, and modes of expression. A definite role in this striking renewal was played by symbolism, which at the end of the nineteenth and the beginning of the twentieth centuries stretched its wing over Ukraine.[41]

A major pre-modernist poet and dramatist who began writing at the end of the nineteenth century was Lesia Ukrainka (real name Larysa Kosach, 1871–1913). Daughter of the populist writer Olena Pchilka (1849–1930) and a niece of the father of Ukrainian democratic socialism, Mykhailo Drahomanov (1841–95), she became the leading writer of her generation. Her first collection of verse, *Na krylakh pisen* (On Wings of Song, 1893), gave but a small foretaste of her later, fiery revolutionary poetry. Her poetic cycle, *Nevilnychi pisni* (The Songs of the Slaves, 1895), justified Franko's famous saying that Lesia Ukrainka was 'more of a man' than anyone else in Ukraine. She overcame her crippling tuberculosis, which ended her life prematurely, by writing inspired, life-affirming poems. Some of them, 'Contra spem spero,' 'Zavzhdy ternovy vinets' (Always a Wreath of Thorns), 'Slovo chomu ty ne tverdaia krytsia' (Word, Why Are You Not like Tempered Steel?), have become examples of the finest Ukrainian poetry since Shevchenko. Her lyrical talent was thus assessed by the editor of her first collected works:

Two sources of creativity lie in Lesia's soul. One, which she cultivated and tempered throughout the long struggle of her life, is the element of true rev-olution, a rejection of tradition, a struggle not for life but for death and a limitless dedication to revolutionary ideals in their romantic form. This pro-vided Lesia's deep lyricism with fiery themes calling for obstinate struggle with the slogan 'kill me – I'll not yield.' This part of Lesia Ukrainka's poetry will not lose its interest for a long time ... Side by side with these fiery calls there is a long row of poems with an open admission of her weakness and pow-erlessness and the sorrow this caused her.[42]

Much greater is Lesia Ukrainka's achievement as a dramatist. She wrote several dramatic poems – *Oderzhyma* (A Possessed Woman), *Kassandra*, *Orhiia* (Orgy), *Na ruinakh* (On the Ruins), *Vavylonsky polon* (The Babylonian Captivity), *Na poli krovy* (On the Field of Blood), *U pushchi* (In the Wilderness) – as well as plays – *Blakytna troianda* (The Azure Rose, 1896), *Rufin i Pristsilla* (Rufinus and Priscilla, 1906), *Boia-rynia* (The Boiar's Wife, 1910), *Lisova pisnia* (A Forest Song, 1911), and *Kaminny hospodar* (The Stone Host, 1912). She often borrowed her sub-jects from world history and literature. 'In Lesia Ukrainka's plays two aspects seem to blend: the personal and the national on the one hand, and the universal on the other. In her dramas there is nothing personal that does not have universal significance; and the most intimate na-tional problems always find close parallels in the history of other na-tions.'[43]

Mykola Zerov evaluates her two last plays accordingly:

Not until the end of her life did [Lesia Ukrainka] come to grips with real drama. *The Stone Host* and *A Forest Song* are dramas in the fullest sense of the word. Here, the depth of ideas, the sparkling dialogue, the variety of themes and motifs, the psychological significance of the characters are supplanted by move-ment, diversity of action, and the visual beauty of the scenes. Lesia Ukrainka's plays represent the highest point in the development of Ukrainian drama. In all of our literature there is nothing more powerful and stage-worthy than *The Stone Host* and *A Forest Song*.[44]

One of Lesia Ukrainka's plays, *The Boiar's Wife*, because of its strong anti-Russian bias, was banned in Soviet Ukraine and was excluded from publication until 1989. Lesia Ukrainka also left some literary criticism and a remarkable collection of private letters. In a letter to Kobylianska she 'did not wish to lay down my arms and renounce the neoromantic flag.'[45]

Of the modernist women prose writers the most prominent was Olha Kobylianska (1863–1942). Born and bred in Bukovina, she was under strong German influence. Some of her early short stories and sketches ('Valse Mélancolique,' 1898) were modernist *par excellence*. Her first novels, *Liudyna* (A Human Being, 1894) and *Tsarivna* (Princess, 1896), were feminist in spirit. Mykola Ievshan thus characterized her early work:

In [Kobylianska's] works a new, ideal sphere is opened to us, giving a view into a new land, where the human spirit is cleansed of earthly dust and finds refuge from the stormy waves of life. Here we are bereft of all hope and aspiration and only one passion awakens in us: to rise ever higher on the scale of perfection, to sculpt one's own soul so that it may shine with beauty and burn with ardent love. We turn away from everyday cares burdening our soul and begin rather to listen to the inner voice in which there beats eternity's pulse. In sacrificing ourselves we do not see any debasement; on the contrary, we are happy, since in reverence to the ideals of love and beauty we see the beginning of a new kingdom, when new life will begin for the individual with the possibility of the harmonious development of all our spiritual forces.[46]

Apart from modernist short stories Kobylianska also wrote two fine novels with a village setting: *Zemlia* (The Earth, 1902) and *V nediliu rano zillia kopala* (On Sunday Morning She Dug for Herbs, 1909). The latter work 'is not epic, but lyric or lyric-epic, it is not "prose," which demands observations and thought about life, but "poetry," rhythmical images in which, first of all, we hear a voice with a typical composition of lyrical verse or a ballad.'[47]

Zemlia was regarded by Franko as Kobylianska's best work. Unfortunately, Kobylianska was heavily influenced by popular German literature (E. Marlitt) of the type represented by the magazine *Gartenlaube*. Many of her novels, such as *Cherez kladku* (Across the Footbridge, 1912), fall into the category of sentimental literature.

The woman who persuaded Kobylianska to start writing in Ukrainian rather than in German, Natalia Kobrynska (1851–1920), was herself a writer. Her symbolist stories 'Dusha' (Soul, 1898) and 'Rozha' (The Rose, 1899) appeared in a magazine. In 1901 she published an essay on August Strindberg. Kobrynska also wrote realistic stories – for example, *Zadlia kuska khliba* (For a Piece of Bread, 1884) – and was the leader of the Ukrainian feminist movement. She was instrumental in publishing a women's almanac, *Pershy vinok* (The First Wreath, 1887).

One of the most original modernist prose writers was Vasyl Stefanyk (1871–1936). The son of a peasant from the region of Pokuttia, he wrote his very short stories in the local dialect. A fellow writer once dubbed Stefanyk 'a poet of peasant despair.' But he is a truly great writer in the expressionist manner. His first collection of short stories, some of them true miniatures, was *Synia knyzhechka* (Little Blue Book, 1899), followed by *Kaminny khrest* (The Stone Cross, 1900), *Doroha* (The Road, 1901), and *Zemlia* (The Earth, 1926). His most creative period came during his student days in Krakow, where he rubbed shoulders with the Polish writers of Mloda Polska (Young Poland). A contemporary review ran as follows:

Stefanyk's works lack conscious reflexes, lack a clear point of view. He coldly outlines the plot, takes in a rich collection of observations of the village and transmutes it with the great warmth of his artistic feeling. The picture he creates is true to life, but is more elevated than an account by a journalist or policeman, because he gives us not only facts and moments but the impression any sensitive man would have if he had observed that scene or character. For him the starting point is an event or condition, but he makes his way deeper into the psychology of the people and thus brings his story to a conclusion. Hence his peasants are barely outlined, but they are psychologically deeply convincing. The artist does not bend his stories to a social doctrine, does not use them to promote anything. He acts as a true artist: he is guided by intuition and feeling ...[48]

Another contemporary comment came from Lesia Ukrainka (1900): 'Stefanyk is not a populist; his *narod* (people) is not the bearer of

"foundations and virtues," which are unknown to "rotten intellectuals." But precisely the absence of these "foundations and virtues,"
disclosed by an able and loving hand, makes a greater and more profound impact on thinking and sensitive readers than all the panegyrics,
full of the best intentions, to the idealized people in populist literature.'[49]

An older writer, the greatest Ukrainian impressionist, was Mykhailo
Kotsiubynsky (1864–1913). He began as a realist with 'Andrii Soloveiko'
(1884) and 'Dlia zahalnoho dobra' (For the Common Good, 1895). Gradually, however, he forsook the realistic story in favour of short impressionist psychological sketches such as 'Na kameni' (On the Rock, 1902),
'Tsvit iabluni' (The Apple Blossom, 1902), and 'Intermezzo' (1908). He
is also the author of two outstanding short novels, *Fata Morgana* (1903–10)
and *Tini zabutykh predkiv* (Shadows of Forgotten Ancestors, 1911). The
first is set during a peasant rebellion in a village, the second among
the Hutsuls in the Carpathian mountains. Bohdan Rubchak's comments
are illuminating:

Fata Morgana, Kosiubynsky's largest work, is built around a confrontation between the two kinds of dreams. Each of the peasant heroes plays out the drama
of his own dream against the tragic panorama of public events (peasant unrest
around 1902). Some of those dreams are enslaving delusions; others are lib-
erated acts of intentionality toward the distant horizons of the future. All fail
equally, the self-deluded dreamers destroying the self-chosen dreamers, to be
destroyed in their turn by the punishing hand of the world.

Andrii Volyk, a peasant whose healthy roots in his native soil have been
damaged by false dreams of progress in a corrupt society, deludes himself by
reveries of a burnt-out factory – a vodka distillery which by its very function
symbolizes false dreams – rising from its ashes like the phoenix and providing
good jobs for everyone in the neighbourhood. Fate sets out to confound Andrii's
dreams in a series of cynical paradoxes ... Volyk's wife, Malanka, who, possibly
by virtue of being a woman, is intimately close to the earth, opposes her
husband's sterile dream by her own reverie of seeding and fruition ... But her
own dream, too, has been corrupted by childish greed and a naive faith in the
powers that be; any day now, she hopes, the landowners will generously
distribute the land to the peasants ... Their daughter, Hafiika, and her young
friend, Marko Hushcha, on the other hand, are constructive dreamers ... they
prove to be as futile as those of their parents.[50]

...

It seems to me that *Shadows* outgrows its 'pastoral' and sociological aspects, although admittedly it does carry traces of both. The meticulously researched and detailed background should not be taken for more than what it is: a dynamic canvas that serves as a backdrop for Kotsiubynsky's triangular structure of opposing forces – the poet's thirst for the ultimate horizons of existence, catalized by an outside source of inspiration, versus the cruelly inhibiting horizons of the world.[51]

A writer who, because of his innovations in the novel and in drama belongs to the modernist camp, was Volodymyr Vynnychenko (1880–1951). His first short story, 'Krasa i syla,' (Beauty and Strength, 1902), showed his powers as an observer of both proletarian and bourgeois milieus. Many of his stories are realistic recreations of life in Ukrainian cities. His first play, *Dyzharmoniia* (Disharmony), appeared in 1906. It propagated Vynnychenko's new morality, which he called 'honesty with oneself.' A novel with that title appeared in 1907. Many other plays followed, some of them gaining an international reputation: *Velyky molokh* (The Great Moloch, 1907), *Bazar* (Market-place, 1910), *Brekhnia* (A Lie, 1910), *Chorna pantera i bily medvid* (Black Panther and White Bear, 1911). 'Vynnychenko maintains in his plays that bourgeois morality also prevails among those who fight the established order, that they, too, are dominated by low instincts and passions. By preaching "honesty with oneself" Vynnychenko wanted to remove this fatal disharmony by preaching that the immoral is moral, and by justifying everything committed by his heroes driven by sheer egoism. In place of the old "bourgeois morality" he substituted an open declaration of amorality.'[52]

Vynnychenko is also the author of several novels, the best of them being *Zapysky kyrpatoho Mefistofelia* (Notes of a Pug-Nosed Mephistopheles, 1917). His novels have been assessed as follows: 'Vynnychenko's novels are full of movement, dynamism, unexpected episodes in which the author forces us to believe; they are devoid of the elegiac meditations or intellectual reflections that we find in Kotsiubynsky. Vynnychenko's novels have interesting plots, intrigues, and, despite their paradoxes, are never dull. His artistic style is fragmentary, energetic, vivid in its originality, although not always refined, but rather flamboyant and unfinished. This is a typically impressionistic style.'[53]

Vynnychenko continued writing after emigrating in 1920. His Utopian novel, *Soniashna mashyna* (The Solar Machine), appeared in 1928. He envisaged a future when the machine would make work unnecessary. His works were very popular in Ukraine in the 1920s. Afterwards they were banned because of his earlier participation in the nationalist government of the Ukrainian People's Republic in 1918–19. He was rehabilitated in 1988.

In 1902 Lesia Ukrainka wrote in a private letter that 'Iatskiv is the most fashionable belles-lettres writer in Galicia ... He writes rather unevenly, sometimes very well, sometimes strangely but more often beautifully.'[54] Mykhailo Iatskiv (1873–1961) was a member of the Young Muse and wrote modernistic short stories. His collections are: *V tsarstvi satany* (In the Kingdom of Satan, 1900), *Z poezii v prozi* (From Poetry in Prose, 1901), *Kazka pro persten* (Fable of the Ring, 1907), *Chorni kryla* (Black Wings, 1909), and *Blyskavytsi* (Lightning, 1912). He is also the author of the novels *Ohni horiat* (Fires Are Burning, 1902) and *Tanets tinei* (The Dance of the Shadows, 1916). Some critics – for example, Lukianovych – thought his modernism was merely 'decorative.' It is true that alongside the modernist there was also a realist writer in Iatskiv, and some of his stories have a certain sociological interest.

Another major talent was Hnat Khotkevych (1877–1938), who began as a modernist with *Poeziia v prozi* (Poetry in Prose, 1902). He is remembered chiefly for his realistic novel set among the Hutsuls, *Kaminna dusha* (A Soul of Stone, 1911), in which sex is seen as a major force in human action. While Iatskiv lived to accept the Soviet occupation, Khotkevych perished during the purges of the 1930s. He has been posthumously rehabilitated and republished. Khotkevych left very acute observations on the development of Ukrainian literature in the first decade of the century: 'The reason for the poverty of our contemporary literature lies in our own poverty, in the illiteracy and backwardness of our nation, in its political lawlessness, and in the lack of culture among out intelligentsia.'[55]

Yet this judgment seems too harsh if we consider the total impact of literary modernism. A few years after Khotkevych wrote these words, almost the contrary could have been said about Ukrainian literature: that it had matured to a remarkable degree. From our discussion so far, it is clear that the definition of modernism, which was a vital new force, expanded beyond the usual interpretation and included all those

works and writers who broke away from the realist-populist tradition
and were innovators in many new directions. Very few writers or works
in Ukrainian literature were in the strict sense of the word, 'modernist.'
Very few took the hint from that prophet of modernity, Nietzsche, who
'pursued everything to the end: the world generated no meaning and
no distinction between good and evil. Reality was pointless ...'[56]

Reality, for Ukrainian writers, was rooted in the debatable status of
the Ukrainian language. Although in 1905 the Russian Academy of
Sciences granted the language separate status, many Ukrainian writers
clung to the romantic idea of the literary language as being close to
the language of the peasants. The positivist trend of the late nineteenth
century, moreover, stressed the importance of writing in a language
that could be understood by the peasants.[57] Modernism revolutionized
the Ukrainian literary language by introducing many new, foreign elements. This prevented Ukrainian from becoming a 'language for do-
mestic use only,' as Kostomarov and others had advocated. But
linguistically and thematically the romantic and positivist ideals lin-
gered on. One must, therefore, turn to those writers in the early twentieth century who continued the traditions of the nineteenth century.
Most of them espoused the well-established realist and populist models
of the past.

Traditionalism

A giant figure among these writers is that of Ivan Franko (1856–1916),
whose literary career began in the late nineteenth century but continued well into the twentieth. Franko's genius was manifold: he was a
prominent activist in socialist and radical circles, and he was a journalist, a scholar, a literary critic, and a writer in all three genres –
poetry, prose, and drama. Friendly with Drahomanov, he yet came to
believe in a free and independent Ukraine, a belief that he expressed
in 'Poza mezhamy mozhlyvoho' (Beyond the Bounds of the Possible,
1900), which the Soviet editors have excluded from his works. The son
of a village blacksmith, he considered himself an ordinary 'worker of
the pen' and laboured tirelessly until in 1908 a serious illness turned
him into a semi-invalid. His collected works have recently been published in fifty volumes, albeit in heavily censored form.

By 1900 Franko was an established writer. In 1900 he published a novel, *Perekhresni stezhky* (Cross-Paths), and in 1907 another *Velyky shum* (The Great Roar), both of them realistic in style, but with strong overtones of a thriller. In 1905 the appearance of his *Boryslavski opovidannia* (Tales from Boryslav) showed his constant social concern.

French naturalism did not have any influence on Franko until his first stories and novels appeared. Even then, after he became familiar with it, this influence was not so strong that it is possible to consider Franko a follower of the naturalist school. What Franko particularly noticed in naturalism had existed in a subdued form in our populist novels: the depiction of a social milieu. But Franko thought of a social milieu as a citizen who wants to participate and influence it. The true naturalists observed the social process as researchers who did not want to spoil things by taking up a personal attitude.[58]

In 1905 Franko published his splendid long poem *Moisei* (Moses). Based on a biblical theme, it discussed in philosophical terms the problem of national leadership. George Shevelov puts the poem in the context of Franko's creative work:

The year 1905 was, in Franko's life, a year of reckoning between life and death, a year of overcoming doubts and vacillations, going beyond the bounds of the possible and leading not in an intended direction but giving content to a man's and a nation's life and creating the highest good – spiritual values. As the doomed Kotsiubynsky wrote in his last works about the glory of life, so did Franko, in his tetralogy *Moses* (poetry), 'Soichyne krylo' (Jay's Wing, prose), 'Pid oborohom' (Under a Haystack, memoirs), and 'Odverty lyst do halytskoi ukrainskoi molodizhi' (An Open Letter to Ukrainian Galician Youth, journalism). The highest achievement of this tetralogy is *Moses* ... The intertwining of the three aspects alone – the personal, the social, and the philosophic – makes *Moses* one of the peaks of Ukrainian literature. On the formal side, too, the poem towers above the poetry of its time and often over all the rest of Franko's poetry.[59]

Some of the earlier poetry of Franko was attuned to symbolism: *'Ziviale lystia* (Withered Leaves, 1896) for long remained the collection that would attract readers of a new generation. From the point of view of composition this is a most compact cycle, and the most varied as to form. This lyrical confession with overtones of dejection and despair was more forceful than the hymn 'Vichny revoliutsioner' (The Eternal Revolutionary), which is good programmatic verse, suitable for martial music.'[60]

Realist writers continued writing after 1900. In that year Borys Hrinchenko (1863–1910) published a novel about village life, *Sered temnoi nochi* (During a Dark Night), showing not so much the 'class struggle' among the peasants as the all-pervasiveness of a criminal mentality. A continuation of this novel was *Pid tykhymy verbamy* (Under the Quiet Willow Trees, 1901), pleading for more enlightenment in the village.

The doyen of populist writers, Ivan Nechui-Levytsky (1838–1918) wrote in 1900 a short novel *Bez puttia* (Senseless), a bitter satire on the decadent movement. The hero and heroine end up in a lunatic asylum. Three years later he wrote a melodramatic tale, set in a village, *Na gastroliakh v Mykytianakh* (Guest Appearances in Mykytiany, published in 1911). In 1902 another older writer, Mykhailo Starytsky (1840–1904), the author of popular historical novels, wrote the novel *Bezbatchenko* (Fatherless, published in 1908) on the agony of illegitimacy. Panas Myrny (1849–1920) continued writing populist stories and plays after 1900.

Three short-story writers stand out for their contribution to Ukrainian realism. They are Stepan Vasylchenko (1878–1932), Les Martovych (1871–1916), and Marko Cheremshyna (real name Ivan Semaniuk, 1874–1927). Vasylchenko's highly poetic prose often recreates the world of children; Martovych is a master of depicting the materialist outlook of the peasants, and Cheremshyna, like Stefanyk, is at his best in psychological sketches of peasants. 'Cheremshyna – a lyricist at heart, in the sense that he seizes on individual moments in life and can enjoy them whether they are pleasant or unpleasant, and wishes only to preserve them before they vanish. What appears to us an "epic" quality is not the result of a balanced view of the world in which he lives but rather of accommodation with that world, which is presented to us without any explanation.'[61]

A prose writer of some importance was Osyp Makovei (1867–1925), who was a protégé of Ivan Franko. He was the author of a series of short stories (*Nashi znakomi*, Our Acquaintances, 1901), the novel *Zalissia* (1897), depicting the life of a clergyman in an impoverished village, and the historical novel *Iaroshenko* (1905). He earned his meagre living as a writer and editor for *Bukovyna*. His often satirical stories are of great value as a portrait of his times.

One of the central themes of Makovei's prose was the life of the Galician bourgeoisie. The world of petty, egotistical private interests, of superstition in everyday life, of respect for official ranks, of careerism, of neglect of civic duties – all this was reflected in many stories, sketches, and feuilletons by Makovei. He knew the bourgeois milieu very well. He looked at it from a distance, but from within, and penetrated deeply into the world of fantasies and conceptions of his heroes – merchants, officials, the clergy, and the intelligentsia.[62]

A writer who in his youth flirted with modernism – in a collection of short stories, *Strazhdannia molodoi liudyny* (Sufferings of a Young Person, 1901) – but who later turned to realism was Antin Krushelnytsky (1878–1941). In 1898–1918 he wrote a novel *Budenny khlib* (Daily Bread), in a strange mixture of styles. He is best remembered for the novel *Rubaiut lis* (Woodcutting, 1914), in which the rich exploiters assume giant proportions. In the 1920s Krushelnytsky migrated to Soviet Ukraine, where, later, he was arrested. He has since been rehabilitated and republished. Another minor though not insignificant writer was Arkhyp Teslenko (1882–1911), who spent long periods of time in jail because of his revolutionary activity. He is the author of many laconic short stories of peasant life and of a long story, *Strachene zhyttia* (A Lost Life, 1910), in which the heroine is driven to suicide.

Four poets in the traditionalist camp deserve to be mentioned. Volodymyr Samiilenko (1864–1925), a talented translator of Homer and Dante, was best-known for his humorous verses. His poems were collected in the volume *Ukraini* (For Ukraine, 1906). Mykola Cherniavsky (1868–1946) was praised by Ievshan for his 'warm lyricism, altruistic urges ... and idealism.'[63] Among his many collections of poetry were *Donetski sonety* (The Donets Sonnets, 1898) and *Zori* (Stars, 1903). His works were banned by the Soviets in the 1930s, after he was arrested. He was posthumously rehabilitated.

Two women wrote lyrical verse: Khrystia Alchevska (1882–1932), the author of *Tuha za sontsem* (Longing for the Sun, 1906), and Uliana Kravchenko (real name Iuliia Shnaider, 1860–1947), the author of the collection *Prima vera* (1885). Unfortunately Kravchenko was rather unproductive in her later years.

Finally, Oleksander Kozlovsky (1876–98) was a poet of promise. His only collection of verse, *Mirty i kyparysy* (Myrtles and Cypresses), was published posthumously in 1905, with a laudatory preface by Ivan Franko.

The contest between traditionalists and modernists was ultimately resolved to the advantage of the latter. Andrii Nikovsky wrote in 1912 that 'Ukraine has a right to a higher culture and follows the path that is destined for her ... Ukrainian literature has gone far beyond the Ukrainian public.'[64] Yet, although outdistanced, the traditionalists continued to exist and to appeal to a wide readership. This bifurcation of literary development continued well into the twentieth century.

So deeply ingrained was the populist notion that literature ought to serve the people that any departure from it was sometimes regarded as an act of national betrayal. Iefremov could not conceive of literature as independent from social and national life, yet the modernists often tried to reach an independent position. They did so in the name of 'beauty' and 'art,' both elusive qualities for the populists. This dichotomy lasted far into the twentieth century. It was resolved by the revolution of 1917, which turned out to be an event of political rather than literary importance.

2   The Failed Revolution   1917–32

Most Ukrainian intellectuals, on the eve of the 1917 revolution, desired more freedom and cultural autonomy for their country. Some went further and pleaded for political independence. However, the Ukrainian population as a whole was given over to either apathy or anarchy. After the downfall of tsarism in February 1917, Ukrainians formed a committee, *Tsentralna Rada* (Central Rada), which soon assumed the trappings, if not the powers, of a government. The revolution in Ukraine was fought primarily for national liberation, though, in fact, civil war prevailed, with the nationalist, Bolshevik, White, and anarchist forces fighting one another. After many changes of government, and the proclamation of an independent Ukrainian People's Republic in January 1918, the country was overrun by the Russian Red army; a Soviet Ukrainian government came to power in 1919. The nationalist forces failed to gain wide support, especially after Lenin promised Soviet Ukraine linguistic and cultural autonomy.

The bloody internecine strife, a national reawakening, and social upheaval left an indelible mark on the Ukrainian history of that era. Despite an inability to develop its own infrastructure, the leaders of the People's Republic, among whom were the historian Hrushevsky and the writer Vynnychenko, showed a definite nucleus of pluralistic party politics. However difficult it may have been in wartime, modern Ukrainian democracy has its roots in the revolution. The failure of a national revolution was followed a few years later by the failure of the Soviet socialist revolution, when despite a military victory, Party centralism put an end to the early tendency towards 'all power to the soviets.' The beginning of Soviet totalitarianism goes back to Lenin's policy of supreme one-party rule, including the establishment of the Cheka, and the propagation of class hatred. True, in 1921, forced by economic collapse, Lenin initiated the New Economic Policy (NEP), which was 'a temporary compromise with capitalism,' allowing some private enterprise and initiative. In the realm of culture the NEP period (1921–8) coincided with liberalization and relative tolerance. Yet even during the liberal era of the 1920s the Communist Party made no secret of the fact that it wanted art and literature to promote its ideology.

In Ukraine various literary groups, from Hart (Tempering) to Proletcult served this purpose. The favoured 'proletarian writers' were not necessarily of working-class origin, but were mouthpieces for party ideology. Following the 1925 Party resolution on literature, various groups, among them the apolitical 'fellow-travellers,' were allowed to flourish. In Ukraine this policy coincided with the so-called Ukrainization, an attempt to introduce the Ukrainian language into the state administration.[1] This provided an added stimulus for Ukrainian literature. The Ukrainian language was now firmly established in the educational system, and some learned institutions – for example, the Academy of Sciences – created during the war of liberation were allowed to grow and develop. All in all, the atmosphere of the late 1920s was very conducive towards the development of literature. Some Bolsheviks who were at the same time Ukrainian patriots, such as Shumsky and Skrypnyk, were in positions of real power, and many indigenous Ukrainian socialists (former Borotbists or Ukapists) held key posts in the press, for example, Ellan Blakytny. A decade of relative non-interference by the Party in literature produced some of the liveliest literary debates and finest literary achievements.

With the collapse of the nationalist forces in 1919 some writers, among them Oles, Vorony, and Vynnychenko, left Ukraine for the West, but those who stayed by and large continued the modernist tradition of innovation and experimentation. Symbolism, which had many adherents in Russia, was best represented in Ukraine by Pavlo Tychyna (1891–1967). His first collection of poems, *Soniashni kliarnety* (The Sunny Clarinets, 1918), is his best. Apart from superb nature lyrics, it contained several poems about the revolution, the last poem 'Zoloty homin' (The Golden Echo) being a lyrical meditation on fratricidal strife and national spontaneity. There followed the brooding *Zamist sonetiv i oktav* (Instead of Sonnets and Octaves, 1920), *Pluh* (The Plough, 1920), and *Viter z*

Ukrainy (Wind from Ukraine, 1924), all of them accomplished collections of introspective and metaphysical verse. One of the warmest and most perceptive assessments of the early Tychyna came, oddly enough, from the old populist, Iefremov, in his history of Ukrainian literature.

What Tychyna has given our literature indeed constitutes a great treasure. It so happened that this young dreamer, with a look directed deep inside him, in his very first book appears so profoundly original and mature and at the same time so tied to the best traditions of our literature that there could be no doubt that a new, fresh, and captivating page has been written in it. Tychyna took from the old soil a humane treatment of themes, a deep national colouring, and the most beautiful language, [forming] a laconic style that in its simplicity, lyricism, and compactness reminds us of the manner of our great prose writer, Vasyl Stefanyk. Possibly of world stature, Tychyna through his form is a deeply national poet because he has used what was best in earlier generations. He drank in, as it were, all the beauty of the popular language and has used it with great taste and mastery in a most sophisticated manner. He has added to this his dreaminess and depth, brilliant form, and a flexible sonorous verse technique, usually scorned by our writers with the exception of two or three mannerist poets.[2]

Ideological interpretations of the early Tychyna poems range from the Soviet left (Leonid Novychenko[3]) to Christian right (Vasyl Barka[4]), but they tell us little about his inimitable poetry. In the late twenties and early thirties this saintly poet, under the pressure of every-increasing controls, underwent a deep change. His early prophecy about 'kissing the Pope's slipper' came true, and the new Tychyna, bereft of his poetic powers, became a Stalinist bard (see page 58).

Ukrainian futurism began before the revolution and is associated with one poet. Mykhail Semenko (1892–1938). He wrote many collections of verse, the most important being *Derzannia* (Daring, 1914) and *Kobzar* (The Minstrel, 1924). He acquired notoriety as the *enfant terrible* of Ukrainian literature, following his blistering attack on Taras Shevchenko, whose cult he considered to be most damaging to Ukrainian culture. For this he was attacked by Ievshan and Sribliansky as a 'literary idiot,' a traitor to his country, and a plagiarist.[5] Recently, Oleh Ilnytzkyj came to the defence of Semenko:

Semenko's appearance in 1914 symbolized the end of one literary era as well as the beginning of another. His Futurism was the first of the many post-Modernist trends that were consciously committed to revitalizing Ukrainian literature and, in a broader sense, Ukrainian culture. This characteristic makes Futurism and Semenko the forerunners of the 'renaissance' of the 1920s ... The main difference is that Semenko knew and advocated the influence of Europe in its most radical guise. In this respect he may well be considered the most European of his contemporaries, and his movement was one more important indicator of just how innovative Ukrainian literature became between 1914 and 1930.[6]

Semenko was arrested and later shot in 1938. His rehabilitation has been only partial.

An associate of Semenko, especially on the journal *Nova generatsiia* (New Generation), was the futurist poet Geo Shkurupii (1903–43), who was also a successful prose writer. Doroshkevych wrote: 'It seems that nowhere except in Shkurupii's [works] can one see the unhealthy psychology of a suburban bourgeois, spoilt by the streets of a large city. While Semenko lived in a world of the decent bohemian café, Shkurupii loves the capitalist city with its parasols, 'blind lampposts,' made-up women, and other characteristics. Only in this way can we explain his 'hymns' – among them a hymn to a 'greasy sausage' to which one of his heroes 'prays fanatically, pressing his nose against the window pane.'[7]

Shkurupii shared Semenko's fate in the Gulag. He has been partially rehabilitated.

Maksym Rylsky (1895–1964) was a modernist who was first published in *Ukrainska khata*. After the revolution he, along with Mykola Zerov, Pavlo Fylypovych, Mykhailo Drai-Khmara, and Osvald Burkhardt, participated in the so-called neoclassicist group, which sometimes tried to emulate the French Parnassians. Rylsky's first collection of poems, *Na bilykh ostrovakh* (On the White Islands, 1910), was followed by *Pid osinnimy zoriamy* (Under the Autumn Stars, 1918), *Synia dalechin* (Sky-blue Distance, 1922), and *Trynadsiata vesna* (The Thirteenth Spring, 1925). Once more, Doroshkevych nicely sums up these early poems:

The poet loves life, but in a static form, he loves the land and sees here a higher harmony ... The catastrophic era of capitalist wars and revolution has not touched the themes of the collections in the least ... The genre frame of the poems recreates the traditions of Pushkin's school, and the subtle aestheticism and Epicureanism, apart from the classical forms, constitute the main stream, which is called neoclassicism. The style, saturated with full, rich images, brilliant, sunny metaphors, and fragrant epithets, as well as the laconic phrase – all these elevate his second collection high in Ukrainian poetry. This is aided by his metric virtuosity, especially in the sonnet form.[8]

Rylsky's early poems are perhaps the only genuine neoclassicist works. Later, in the 1930s, he followed Tychyna's path, changing his outlook and style according to Party dictates.

In his penetrating article 'The Legend of Ukrainian Neoclassicism'[9] George Shevelov argues that some of the neoclassicists – for example, Drai-Khmara and Fylypovych – were simply symbolists and that even the maître of the group, Mykola Zerov (1890–1937), hid behind a facade of classicism. Zerov, who was a professor of literature at Kiev University, published translations – Antolohiia rymskoi poezii (An Anthology of Roman Poetry, 1920) and a collection Kamena (Camena, 1924). He was better-known for his scholarly works, such as Nove ukrainske pysmenstvo (New Ukrainian Literature, 1924) and for critical essays in Do dzherel (To the Sources, 1926) and Vid Kulisha do Vynnychenka (From Kulish to Vynnychenko, 1928). Shevelov believes that Zerov's best poetry has only a shell of classicism:

The hard form of classicism, a stand above all things and time – was a refuge from the poet's feeling of disillusionment, loneliness, the world's illusoriness, man's meanness and loss of faith, which was his deepest reaction to the brutal and dirty reality of his day. Zerov was not a neoclassicist in the full sense of the term; he searched for classicism and desperately yearned for it, but only infrequently did he reach a classical harmony not only of word and form but also of outlook. More often than not the symmetrical form masked and stilled the cry of his tormented soul.[10]

Zerov certainly had a premonition of the terror that claimed his life in the Gulag. His collections, Sonnetarium (Munich, 1948), Catalepton (Philadelphia, 1951), and Corollarium (Munich, 1958), were published posthumously, along with his lectures on the history of Ukrainian literature, which appeared in Canada in 1977. He was rehabilitated in 1966.

Pavlo Fylypovych (1891–1937) was the author of two collections of poems, *Zemlia i viter* (Earth and Wind, 1922) and *Prostir* (Space, 1925), as well as several scholarly studies. Like Zerov and Drai-Khmara, he lived among academics in Kiev. All three ended their careers in the Gulag.

Fylypovych wrote symbolist poems even in 1925 [writes Shevelov] but his attraction to neoclassicism grew stronger all the time. While neoclassicism is negligible in *Zemlia i viter*, it sets the tone in *Prostir* ... Partly, his symbolism contained kernels of neoclassicism. In a typically symbolist poem 'Na potalu kaminnym kryham' (Defying the Stone Boulders), the poet wrote about himself:

> I give up my anxious soul
> And the cold calmness of thought ...

and the last component, which no symbolist need stress – the 'cold calmness of thought' – appeared very clearly in the symbolist poems of Fylypovych, later dominating his poetry and distancing it from 'the anxious soul.'[11]

Mykhailo Drai-Khmara (1889–1939) published a collection of poems, *Prorosten* (Young Shoots, 1926), and a monograph on Lesia Ukrainka. His poem about the neoclassicists, 'Lebedi' (The Swans, 1928), earned him years of incarceration. His *Letters from the GULAG* (New York, 1983) was published after his official rehabilitation.

Like the neoclassicists, another group of writers, Lanka (The Link), were officially classed as 'fellow-travellers.' This misnomer, invented by Trotsky, put all the writers who wished to avoid politics into one convenient category, ascribing to them left leanings that none of them in fact had. Lanka's most prominent prose writer was Valeriian Pidmohylny (1901–41), who became a major novelist in the 1920s. He was the author of many short stories and the novels *Ostap Shaptala* (1922), *Misto* (The City, 1928), and *Nevelychka drama* (English translation, *A Little Touch of Drama*, 1930). Pidmohylny was also a translator of French literature, which in turn influenced him. A dissertation has been written on Pidmohylny and Maupassant.[12]

From his very earliest works to his last, Pidmohylnyj consistently focuses his attention on instinctual, sexual, and creative energies. In the cluster of thematic motifs that characterize his work, particularly the early works, these energies are associated with revolutionary anarchism, hunger, dreamy romanticism, the night, and especially, the steppe. This thematic cluster, defined earlier as the magic of the night, is essentially parallel to the Dionysian version of Nietzsche's Will to Power. The association becomes more precise in the two novels, where the differentiation between the magic of the night and its polar complement, reason, is most acutely delineated. But the two novels are not thematically identical. Where in *Misto* Pidmohylnyj saw or at least envisioned the possibility of a harmony or unity between the two forces, in *Nevelycka drama* the possibility is gone ... In his last novel Pidmohylnyj has moved beyond Nietzsche to an existential position that no longer allows for idealized harmony or transcendent affirmation.[13]

Like so many of his contemporaries, Pidmohylny perished in the Gulag. He was in the midst of his literary career. In 1988 he was tentatively rehabilitated.

Another member of Lanka was a major poet, Ievhen Pluzhnyk (1898–1936). He was the author of the collections *Dni* (Days, 1926), *Rannia osin* (Early Autumn, 1927), and *Rivnovaha* (Equilibrium, 1933). He also wrote a novel, *Neduha* (Illness, 1928), and some plays. '[Pluzhnyk] was a dreamer who was ashamed of his dreaminess. A poet who did not believe in his poetry ... Hence the solitude. The solitude of a recluse? On the contrary, the solitude of one who wants to be with people ... And there is another striking feature of this lonesome man who loves people: the hope in the future, which, at times, reaches something like a mystical ecstasy.'[14]

Sensing the changes of political climate Pluzhnyk attempted to elevate Communism in his poetry. But to no avail. He was arrested, and died in the Solovky Islands. He has been rehabilitated and republished.

A minor expressionist poet, Todos Osmachka (1895–1962) was also a member of Lanka. His collections were *Krucha* (Precipice, 1922), *Skytski ohni* (Scythian Fires, 1925), and *Klekit* (The Gurgling, 1929). To avoid arrest he feigned insanity. After The Second World War he went to the United States, where he re-emerged as a writer (see pages 96, 98–9).

A talented prose writer and member of Lanka (later of MARS) was Borys Antonenko-Davydovych (1899–1984). He was the author of the play *Lytsari absurdu* (The Warriors of the Absurd, 1924) and collections

of short stories and sketches: *Zaporosheni syluety* (The Dusty Silhou-
ettes, 1925), *Synia voloshka* (The Blue Cornflower, 1927), and *Zemleiu
ukrainskoiu* (Across the Ukrainian Land, 1930). His novel *Smert* (Death,
1928) became controversial. Antonenko-Davydovych spent more than
two decades in the Gulag and in exile, before being rehabilitated and
republished in the 1950s (see page 76).

A major poet who stood halfway between Lanka and the neoclassicists and who preserved his integrity was Volodymyr Svidzinsky
(1885–1941). He was the author of the collections *Lirychni poezii* (Lyrical
Poems, 1922), *Veresen* (September, 1927), and *Poezii* (Poems, 1940). He
also translated Aristophanes. During the war evacuation in 1941 he was
burned alive in a house set on fire by the Soviet forces. A collection
of his poems, *Medobir* (Honey Hills, 1975), appeared in the West. Svidzinsky has been rehabilitated. Ivan Dziuba wrote of him in 1968:

Silence and loneliness are Svidzinsky's most frequently used concepts, the most
persistent search for conditions of spiritual revelation ... In general his poetry
is quite varied. It is strange that a poet who wrote so little (at least we know
little of what he wrote), who appeared so passive, so estranged from life (a
man stewing in his own juice) could, in fact, be so rich, varied, and multifaceted.
He is, at the same time, a subjective lyricist and skilled at epic verse; sorrowful
meditation and calmness of vision are his as much as existential *angst* ... His
poetry is not so much the poetry of imagination, the energy of feeling, or
metaphoric-associative thinking (although all these elements are present) as
the poetry of observation.[15]

There were many writers who welcomed the revolution and the
Soviet regime and tried to spread optimism about it in their works.
These were often given the name of 'proletarian writers,' though few
of them were of working-class origin. What mattered most was their
dedication to the Communist cause. Among the foremost in this category were the so-called first brave ones (*pershi khorobri*): 'Those in
the forefront of the Ukrainian intelligentsia, the better, the stronger,
and the more consistent, were led from the idea of a national rebirth
by the logic of class struggle to the idea of class liberation, to the forging
of the path of history by the sledgehammer of the proletarian dictatorship. This curved path of history was taken by the pioneers of the

Ukrainian intelligentsia – "the first brave ones" – Mykhailychenko, Zalyvchy, Chumak.'[16]

Vasyl Chumak (1900–19), author of *Zaspiv* (Invocation, 1919), was executed by the Denikin forces. For him the revolution was a new religion: 'Revolution. Socialist. The crisis of concepts and norms. The crisis of religion. Let us smash the old Tablets. We carry the scriptures of the First One to an execution. We must create new concepts and norms immediately. A new religion. The scriptures – a formula for the revolutionary outlook of the proletariat in the struggle for socialism.'[17]

Hnat Mykhailychenko (1892–1919), the author of *Blakytny roman* (The Blue Novel, 1918–19) and several short stories, was also executed by the Denikin forces. His modernistic novel has been called 'a strange synthesis of eroticism and revolution.'[18] His style has no forerunners and no followers. The editor of his works, Hadzinsky, wrote: 'Hnat Mykhailychenko was an idealist, but in a very limited and definite sense, that is, in his demands that a human being be not ordinary but a real human being. Not a *homo sapiens* or *homo homini lupus est*, but a new human being in a new society, which was to be created by revolution. Some Nietzschean type of the "red superman." '[19]

Andrii Zalyvchy, the author of some short stories, was executed in 1918 by the Hetmanite forces. He completes the martyred trio of the first Communist writers.

A proletarian poet of clearly propagandist bent was Vasyl Ellan Bla-kytny (1893–1925), who played a prominent role as editor of *Visti* (News). He was the author of a collection of verse, *Udary molota i sertsia* (Blows of the Hammer and Heart, 1920), and some parodies. Blakytny was the first Ukrainian writer to conceive of an elitist literary organization that he called an 'academy.' After his untimely death, the project was taken over by Mykola Khvylovy, who in 1925 founded VAPLITE, the Vilna Akademiia Proletarskoi Literatury (Free Academy of Proletarian Literature). Under Khvylovy's undisputed leadership till 1927, this organization played a prominent part in uniting many leading writers around a platform of quality literature, while paying lip service to the Communist cause. The Vaplitians, in an apt phrase, 'led Ukrainian literature and the Ukrainian people away from [the constraints] of provincialism and placed them eye-to-eye with the world as an equal partner.'[20] It was this orientation to the West, rather than its later alleged nationalism, that led to the dissolution of VAPLITE in 1928.

Mykola Khvylovy (real name Fitilov, 1893–1933) was not only a charismatic literary personality but a major prose writer and essayist. He was a member of the Communist Party, but believed in an independent Soviet Ukraine, free of Russian influence. His two collections of poems were *Molodist* (Youth, 1921) and *Dosvitni symfonii* (Pre-Dawn Symphonies, 1922). He also published collections of exquisite short stories in the neoromantic tradition: *Syni etiudy* (Blue Etudes, 1923), *Osin* (Autumn, 1924), *Tvory* (Works, 1927), and an unfinished novel, *Valdshnepy* (The Woodcocks, 1927). A contemporary reaction to his works was as follows:

I would call Khvylovy a formless writer. I think this best characterizes his creative work as it stands before us today. In his creative personality there are various, sometimes contradictory, forces, which, like a wild wind, attract and direct him although he ought to be their master. To consider all this from a class point of view, these forces, as we tried to argue, are mostly of a bourgeois character, with a strong tendency towards decadence. This does not mean that Khvylovy is a spokesman for the new bourgeoisie, which is being born in our complex economy. He is the spokesman of disillusion, he doubts if we shall realize, with all our forces, the socialist ideal. Therefore, only indirectly, against his own will, he sadly creates for the benefit of hostile forces.[21]

Khvylovy's disillusionment with the revolution and his profound lyricism led to a great literary achievement.

Khvylovy loved insanely the scent of the word, to use his beloved expression. He wove words into arabesques and patterns, spread them out in funeral processions, mastered them in dancing groups. Sometimes he found Ukrainian words inadequate, he wished for greater contrasts, stronger scented aromas – he borrowed French and Russian words. The purists were angry with him. Poor linguists. Khvylovy loved the scent of words, for words, for him, were not a screen from life or a reflection of life, as the Marxists would have it. They were a part of life. Khvylovy was madly in love with life.[22]

There were parallels to Khvylovy's prose in Russia. 'One can easily find bridges between Khvylovy and Pilniak, Zamiatin, even to Bely, as far as artistic methods and even content are concerned.'[23]

Equally important is Khvylovy's contribution as an essayist, primarily because it initiated the so-called literary discussion (1925–8), the last free public debate on Ukrainian culture in Soviet Ukraine.[24] His collections of essays were *Kamo hriadeshy?* (Whither Are You Going, 1925), *Dumky proty techii* (Thoughts against the Current, 1926), and *Apolohety pysaryzmu* (Apologians of Scribbling, 1927). In these essays Khvylovy boldly criticized the Communist graphomaniacs (red *Prosvita*), and called on Ukrainian writers to turn away from Russia, pointing instead to Western Europe as the source of real culture, invoking the coming of the 'Asiatic Renaissance.' His slogan 'away from Moscow' was, of course, most controversial and provoked a response from Stalin himself:

Khvylovy's demands that the proletariat in Ukraine be immediately de-Russified, his belief that 'Ukrainian poetry should keep as far as possible from Russian literature and style,' his pronouncement that 'proletarian ideas are familiar to us without the help of Russian art,' his passionate belief in some messianic role for the young Ukrainian intelligentsia, his ridiculous and non-Marxist attempt to divorce culture from politics – all this and much more in the mouth of this Ukrainian Communist sounds (and cannot sound otherwise) more than strange. At a time when the Western European proletarian classes and their Communist Parties are full of affection for Moscow, this citadel of the international revolutionary movement, at a time when Western European proletarians look with enthusiasm to the flag that flies over Moscow, this Ukrainian Communist Khvylovy has nothing to say in favour of Moscow except to call on Ukrainian leaders to run away from Moscow as fast as possible. And this is called internationalism.[25]

There is no doubt that Khvylovy's literary policy amounted in the eyes of the Party to a serious political deviation. He was hounded by Communist officials after his work was criticized in many journals and newspapers. Khvylovy tried to elude the attacks and founded a new, avant-garde journal, *Literaturny iarmarok* (Literary Fair, 1929), but in the end, as a gesture of protest, he committed suicide in 1933. His works and ideas were banned until 1988, when he was partially rehabilitated.

The following well-known writers belonged to VAPLITE: Bazhan, Dniprovsky, Dosvitnii, Dovzhenko, Ianovsky, Iohansen, Khvylovy, Kopylenko, Kulish, Senchenko, Slisarenko, Smolych, Sosiura, and Tychyna.

Some of the Vaplitians, like the popular poet Volodymyr Sosiura (1898–1965) were converts to Communism. Early in the revolution Sosiura fought in Petliura's nationalist army, only to go over later to the Bolsheviks. In 1921 he published a collection of verse, *Chervona zyma* (Red Winter), which established him as a 'proletarian' poet. Iakiv Savchenko wrote in 1925:

We shall not make a mistake if we say that Sosiura is the poet of the revolution. He is least influenced, almost uninfluenced by the artistic outlook of the pre-revolutionary era ... He was formed and educated by the revolutionary struggle, which endowed him with the strong integrity of class character ... Sosiura's sociological and psychological foundation is firm. Socially he is tied to the working masses and he is also psychologically with them. He is not split into two, not weakened by the mood and individualistic culture of the previous era.[26]

A different opinion about Sosiura is held by Vasyl Hryshko, who published the poet's banned verses:

One can talk here about a more complex and deeper ambivalence, connected to the serious inner conflict not of an average man but of an active, creative individual, called upon to shape external reality. One can talk about a man, who sincerely and voluntarily chose the Communist ideology, shaping it to his personal and national character and who remains faithful to this ideology whatever its historical metamorphoses. But at the same time this human being tries to be 'honest with himself,' believing deeply in the consonance of his character with his ideology and therefore he is open about himself ... Such a person experiences the point of sharp collision of these two forces and this causes a permanent conflict with Soviet reality ...[27]

Sosiura's inner conflict is most evident in his collection *Sertse* (Heart, 1931). He continued to express it in the 1930s and later (see page 66).

A much less popular but much more original poet was Mykola Bazhan (1904–83), who began writing as a futurist. He was the author of the collections *17-y patrul* (The 17th Patrol, 1926), *Rizblena tin* (The Sculpted Shadow, 1927), *Budivli* (Buildings, 1929), and *Doroha* (The Road, 1930).

What is Bazhan's style? Futurism? Expressionism? Baroque? Romanticism à la Hoffmann? It would be vain to force a master of poetry into other frameworks. True, futurism gave the poet an inner freedom from psychological and aesthetic inertia ... Expressionism gave him the taste of a passionate consciousness, a thirst for life ... The Ukrainian and the Western baroque offered the totality of detail, and the romanticism of Hoffmann and Gogol gave him the expansive world of fantasy ...

Perhaps because of this it is not beauty but force that plays a part in Bazhan's style, the force of the elements, contrasts, and rhythms. And most of all, the force of humanity governed by universal laws.[28]

Already the young Bazhan, who kept well away from politics, may be regarded as one who was inclined towards the powers that be. 'The Vaplitians oriented themselves towards the reactionary romanticism of the West. Bazhan exposed it. The Vaplitians cultivated the idea of eternal conflict between the romantic dream of the artist and reality. Bazhan wrote about the tragic nature of such conflicts. The Vaplitians, lastly, idealized the split man who lives simultaneously in two worlds. Bazhan dreamt of the integrated monolith of the human soul. The poet's challenge to reactionary ideals is clear.'[29] This challenge became much clearer in the 1930s when the publication of Bazhan's fine long poem *Sliptsi* (The Blind Men) was interrupted. Soon afterwards, under official pressure, he went over to 'socialist realism.'

A career similar to that of Bazhan was pursued by the talented prose writer Iurii Ianovsky (1902–54). In the 1920s he distinguished himself through his short stories: *Mamutovi byvni* (The Mammoth's Tusks, 1925) and *Krov zemli* (Blood of the Soil, 1927). 'Ianovsky constructs his stories openly, with all the ''means uncovered'' as the formalists would say. And these artistic means are not directed so much towards construction, as to the destruction of the old form, towards a break with tradition ... Both G. Shkurupii and Iu. Ianovsky were tied to a futurist group of writers, the former still remaining in the group, which helped both writers to free themselves from tradition and become ''Europeanized.'' '[30]

Ianovsky is the author of two romantic novels, *Maister korablia* (The Master of the Ship, 1928) and *Chotyry shabli* (Four Sabres, 1930).

In 1928 Ianovsky published a collection of poetry, *Prekrasna Ut*
(The Most Beautiful Ut, second edition 1932), hoping for a socialist
success (Ut is an acronym for 'Ukraina trudiashchykh,' Ukraine of
the Workers). His novel *Four Sabres* was sharply attacked by the
official critics:

The writer romanticizes in every way the heroes of his novel, and their reckless
behaviour. As part of the idealization of the Zaporozhian Cossacks memories
are offered of the Zaporozhian Sich and its glorious heroes, who are, according
to Ianovsky, the forefathers of his own heroes, whom he sometimes also com-
pares to Napoleon's marshalls, etc. However, the activities of these heroes are
shown without any connection to proletarian leadership. The writer failed to
show the leading and guiding role of the Communist Party in the people's
struggle against the external and internal enemies of the young socialist country.[31]

   A talented prose writer was Oles Dosvitnii (1891–1934). He was an
active member of the Communist Party and travelled to China and the
United States. He wrote the novels *Amerykantsi* (The Americans, 1925),
Khto (Who, 1927), *Nas bulo troie* (There Were Three of Us, 1929), and
many short stories. The satirical novel *The Americans* is 'a book more
interesting as a memoir than as a literary work.'[32]

Has anyone noticed the mastery with which Dosvitnii depicts what might be
called the exotic? Have our critics noticed the beautiful pictures of the 'warm
Korean autumn'? ... Our era is not the time for large epics and compositionally
perfect canvases. Consciously or intuitively Dosvitnii came to this conclusion.
In any case, he advances along a very interesting path ... Was it not Dosvitnii
who gave us a chance to smell the contemporary Orient and Occident? Was
it not he who painted the depths of unknown oceans over which his *Rembrandt*
travels? Was it not he who gave us the entire gallery of travelling revolutionaries?[33]

Despite attempts to conform to the Party line, Dosvitnii was arrested
and perished in the 1930s. He has been rehabilitated.
   Oleksa Slisarenko (1891–1937) started as a futurist poet and later turned
to prose. His collections of poems included *Na berezi kastalskomu* (On
the Castile Shore, 1918), *Poemy* (Poems, 1923), and *Baida* (1928). Among

his prose works were collections of short stories, *Plantatsii* (Plantations, 1925) and *Kaminny vynohrad* (Stone Grapes, 1927), and the novels *Bunt* (Rebellion, 1928) and *Chorny anhel* (The Black Angel, 1929). 'Slisarenko's prose is a very interesting attempt to create a story purely through plot development. Slisarenko is above all a storyteller, a fabulist. His attention is chiefly centred on the moment. From this are derived the specific devices of his creativity. He never clutters the plot with redundant episodes, taking only two or three of them, tying them together through a causal relationship, and leading the plot to a logical conclusion.'[34]

The prose writer Ivan Senchenko (1901–75) may be remembered for one short work. He wrote and rewrote *Chervonohradsky tsykl* (Chervonohrad Cycle, 1929–69), *Solomiansky tyskl* (Solomianka Cycle, 1956–7), and *Donetsky tsykl* (Donetsk Cycle, 1952–64) – all about the Ukrainian working class, but the most remarkable, satirical, and prophetic piece, 'Iz zapysok kholuia' (The Notes of a Flunky), appeared in 1927. This banned piece of writing was recovered in 1988 with the following words:

With pride, cocky self-satisfaction, joyfully and confidently the 'grandiose and incomparable Flunky' lays down his system of flunkyism, the moral-philosophical principles of the conscious depersonalization of man, the renunciation of his own self, the transformation of a personality into a 'cog and wheel' of the social mechanism, the order established by the 'incomparable Pius.' Senchenko's happy, thirty-year old Flunky has a 'strong body, red cheeks, a flexible spine and rubber feet.' The most important task for the Flunky is to solidify the testament of flunkyism, that is: to instil into his children obedience, humility, silence; to spread the system of flunkyism throughout society and mankind and to extirpate from man the Promethean spirit, the need to think and to have one's own opinion. The main thing is to think like everybody else ...[35]

Although severely criticized, Senchenko managed to survive the purges. His early work is his best and was praised by Oleksander Biletsky: '[Senchenko is] a prose writer who struggles with the lyricist in himself, with the poet of moods. The former is always the winner. The impressionistic style deprives characters and events of clarity; the story, designed as a story, is suddenly transformed into a *Stimmungsskiz*, the plot evaporates and the uncertain game between the writer and the reader (à la Khvylovy) ends in a draw.'[36]

A versatile writer, with serious scholarly interests, was Maik Iohansen (1895–1937), the author of collections of poems: *Dhori* (Upwards, 1921), *Revoliutsiia* (Revolution, 1923), *Dorobok* (The Output, 1924), as well as short stories, collected in *17 khvylyn* (17 Minutes, 1925). Iohansen also wrote a parodistic novel, *Podorozh uchenoho doktora Leonardo i ioho maibutnioi kokhanky prekrasnoi Altsesty u slobozhansku Shveitsatiiu* (The Journey of the Learned Doctor Leonardo and His Future Mistress, the Beautiful Alceste, into Slobozhanska Switzerland, 1930). In 1928 he published *Iak buduietsia opovidannia* (How a Short Story Is Built). Here is an evaluation of his early poetry: 'Iohansen is a typical jeweller of sounds, a talented digger in verbal depths, a philologist of poetry. His mastery of alliteration is undisputed. At first he appears to be a refined decadent of the type of Verlaine ... Along the magnetic field of the revolution his verse playthings are no longer playthings; they become inspired figures of social significance.'[37] He was arrested and perished in the Gulag.

Somewhat similar in his style to Iohansen was Leonid Skrypnyk (1893–1929), the author of an experimental, satirical novel, written like a film scenario, called *Inteligent* (The Intellectual, 1929).

A writer who continued in the realist tradition was Petro Panch (1891–1978), who produced several collections of short stories, among them *Solomiany dym* (The Straw Fire, 1925) and *Myshachi nory* (The Burrows of Mice, 1926), and a collection of tales, *Holubi eshelony* (The Blue Echelons, 1928). '[Panch] showed himself to be a talented observer of the new mores in the provinces. His better tales attract by their sheer realism and by an absence of stylistic and ideological hyperbole ... Panch's precise realistic sketches are attuned to the old realistic school, but in the technique of this young writer there is a dynamism and a learned literary manner, lacking in the old literature.'[38]

Today we know that even in those supposedly liberal days Panch and other writers were subjected to severe censorship. In 1990 a Soviet critic wrote that 'Panch has thoroughly "ploughed over" his novel *The Blue Echelons* (1928). He has deleted from it the tragic lyricism of the hero, the captain of the Ukrainian People's Army, Lets-Otamanov.'[39] Similar cuts were made in Holovko's novel *Weeds*. Since some manuscripts of works mutilated in the 1920s have still been preserved, it is hoped that uncensored editions may now be published.

In addition, new demands were being made on the writers.

The dogged question 'either-or' posed by the logic of life backs each of them against the wall, demanding an unequivocal answer (not just a declaration, but in their creative work too) which determines the place of the literary artist in a complex intertwining of social forces. It is then that some writers depart from the revolution, openly castigating its successes or hide themselves behind politically neutral themes, reflecting reality in a crooked mirror, or flee from reality into the world of romantic illusion, while others, on the contrary, set themselves ideologically on the side of the proletariat. Petro Panch belongs to the second category of contemporary Ukrainian writers.'[40]

A writer with a gift for psychological analysis and an inclination towards satire was Hryhorii Epik (1901–37). He was the author of collections of short stories, including *Na zlomi* (The Turning Point, 1926) and *V snihakh* (Amid the Snows, 1928), the novels *Bez gruntu* (Without Ground, 1928) and *Nepiia* (1930), and the collection *Tom satyry* (A Volume of Satire, 1930).

Having gone over to the literary organization VAPLITE, Epik experienced the negative influence of its defective theoretical and aesthetic tendencies. As a result, works like *Nepiia* appeared in which the writer resorts to excessive psychologizing, wallowing in the human psyche, which has lost its true path and has in effect abandoned those ideological principles for which it fought. This person, in Epik's novel, is a Komsomol leader, a district secretary, Marko. His love for the 'nepiia' Rita becomes pathologically antagonistic, leading to a loss of perspective, making him politically blind.[41]

Such 'mistakes' were not forgiven Epik, even when he tried desperately to write the kind of prose that was required. His last two novels, *Persha vesna* (The First Spring, 1931) and *Petro Romen* (1932), failed to please the official critics. The former dealt with collectivization, the latter was written at the request of the Komsomol to 'create a positive type of young worker.' Such demands alone were enough to destroy any serious writer. Soon Epik was arrested and perished in the purges.

Iurii Smolych (1900–16) began his career in the theater. He wrote a novel of adventure, *Ostannii Eidzhvud* (The Last Agewood, 1926), and the Wellsian novel *Hospodarstvo doktora Galvanesku* (The Household of Dr Galvanescu, 1928). Even in the 1920s when this was not obligatory, he betrayed an interest in the unmasking of anti-Soviet activities, shown in *Pivtora liudyny* (One Man and a Half, 1927), which he later developed into a fine art. The target of the novel *Falshyva Melpomena* (The False Melpomene, 1928) was Ukrainian 'bourgeois nationalism,' which became a special preoccupation for Smolych.

Another prose writer of lesser importance was Oleksander Kopylenko (1900–58), the author of a long story, *Buiny khmil* (Wild Hops, 1925), and a novel, *Vyzvolennia* (Liberation, 1929). In the novel, the author's 'disgust with the city of the NEP era deepened, and there is an obvious inclination to counterpose the cleanliness of the steppe and the soil as well as the unspoilt village morality against the dirty city.'[42] Kopylenko was soon criticized for his 'pessimism' and 'individualism,' and he heeded the critics and changed his style. This may have saved his life.

A very different writer, whose works had philosophical overtones, was Arkadii Liubchenko (1899–1945), the author of a collection of short stories, *Buremna put* (Stormy Passage, 1927), and a book of sketches that a critic has called 'a philosophical mystery,' *Vertep* (1930; the title is the Ukrainian word for puppet theatre). In *Vertep* juxtaposed scenes 'outline a basic moral idea – an idea of eternal disquiet and the concomitant idea of Ukraine's messianism. There arises, with great persuasiveness, faith in man and faith in Ukraine, which penetrates the entire *Vertep* as well as the Ukrainian cultural renaissance of the 1920s. Liubchenko's materialism, although this sounds like a paradox, grows out of his faith. It becomes transformed into great idealism.'[43]

Liubchenko refused to be evacuated with other writers during the German invasion. He died in Germany, where he left the archives of VAPLITE, whose secretary he was. The archives have been preserved in the West.

Ivan Dniprovsky (1895–1934) wrote poetry, short stories, and plays. The romantic play *Liubov i dym* (Love and Smoke, 1925) was followed by the revolutionary drama *Iablunevy polon* (Apple Blossom Captivity, 1926). Dniprovsky, whose works were banned after his death, also left some interesting personal letters, which were published posthumously. He died of tuberculosis in Ialta.

A close friend of Dniprovsky, Mykola Kulish (1892–1937), became the greatest Ukrainian playwright of the Soviet era. A prolific writer, he began his career as dramatist with two propagandist plays, *Devianosto sim* (Ninety-Seven, 1924) and *Komuna v stepakh* (A Commune in the Steppes, 1925). However, after becoming a close friend of Les Kurbas, the director of the Berezil theatre, Kulish produced four masterpieces: *Narodny Malakhii* (The People's Malakhii, 1928), *Myna Mazailo* (1929), *Patetychna sonata* (Sonata Pathétique, 1930), and *Maklena Grasa* (1933). Various critics have tried to assess his greatness. According to one of them,

Kulish will enter the history of Ukrainian literature and theatre as the creator of neo-baroque drama. The genesis of his style is very complex. For Kulish the Ukrainian tradition of the *Ninety-Seven* and *Commune in the Steppes* did not reach further than Tobilevych. But later he appropriated the tradition of the Ukrainian *vertep* [puppet theatre] and the treasures of the dramatic poems of Lesia Ukrainka, whose influence may be seen in *Sonata Pathétique*. Kulish grew in the artistic atmosphere of Pavlo Tychyna, Mykola Khvylovy, and Les Kurbas and the Berezil theatre. It was they who pushed him towards the study of European and world drama. Yet master that he was, he copied nothing. In *Khulii Khuryna* Kulish writes that he could not accept the framework of the ancient, Shakespearean, or Molièrean drama, since the material and spirit of his age could not be compressed into it.[44]

George Shevelov warns against any simplistic political interpretation of Kulish:

The theme of Kulish's creativity was how man becomes human. This is a tragic theme and has always been so through the ages. Kulish explored it honestly and profoundly. He offered no solutions, programs, slogans, advice, or prescriptions. His works were not written to answer the question "What Is to Be Done?" He was neither Chernyshevsky nor Lenin. He was without exaggeration a writer of genius, and he knew and sensed that in some cases great helplessness offers a key to great art. He was also a great craftsman able to treat this theme in different ways from the tragi-comic *The People's Malakhii* à la Don Quixote, to the playfulness and humour of *Myna Mazailo*, from the helicons of *Sonata Pathétique* to the elegy of hopelessness in *Maklena Grasa*.[45]

Finally, a Soviet critic, who did much to restore Kulish's good name after his rehabilitation:

With their atmosphere of intellectual dispute Kulish's plays belong to the twentieth century, and the dramatist and his heroes take it for granted that man can think rationally, see the causes and effects of some social tendencies and see them in perspective. At the same time a great deal of Kulish's plays is openly and clearly lyrical. The form of the lyrical drama is born from the recognition of the significance of human emotions as a means of knowing truth, taking into account the complex spiritual world of man and his emotional depth as expressions of humanity. In this respect Kulish's theatre appeals both to reason and to the emotion of the spectators. In his best works 'ratio' and 'emotio' are organically united, addressed to the complete human being and all the means of cognition. From this point of view, Kulish, a sober researcher of social life, carefully analyses his subject while remaining a lyric writer. He offers an example of a rare combination of the contrasting literary gifts.[46]

Despite his efforts to write some conformist plays, Kulish could not avoid arrest. He died in the Gulag. In the 1960s and later in the 1980s he was rehabilitated, but some of his plays remain proscribed.

Kulish's successes and failures were very much tied to the fate of the Berezil theatre, directed by Les Kurbas (1887–1942), who also perished in the Gulag. It was the production by Berezil of *The People's Malakhii* and *Myna Mazailo*, as well as the close friendship between Kulish and Kurbas, that were so important for Kulish the artist.

As the last Vaplitian to be considered here, Kulish epitomized the tragedy of the Ukrainian Communists. A Party member, like Khvylovy and Kurbas, he naively hoped that the Ukrainian Communist Party would be able to protect the Ukrainian literary renaissance. The terror, not fully unleashed until the 1930s, swept away mercilessly both those who were Communists and those who were not, crushing everything showing independence and spontaneity.

Among the non-Communists was a group of writers, diverse in their literary tendencies, who in 1934 faced the firing squad. The most talented of these was Hryhorii Kosynka (1899–1934), the author of several collections of remarkable impressionistic short stories: *Na zolotykh bohiv* (Against the Gods of Gold, 1922), *Maty* (Mother, 1925), and *V zhytakh* (In the Wheatfields, 1926), 'Faust.'

Hryhorii Kosynka has usually been characterized as a dazzling writer, rich in images and rhythm in a work of prose, a cultured writer who simultaneously wrote in a very narrow vein. He was unwilling to widen this vein, being more inclined to probe deeper and improve his artistic insights, and had no fear of repeating certain motifs and psychological sketches ... Kosynka throughout his work is the last follower of the impressionist Ukrainian village short story. He is, however, a forceful follower and develops what he found in Stefanyk, Vasylchenko, and, in part, in Kotsiubynsky, at a time when new social themes were developing directly contrary to this trend in Ukrainian literature.[47]

Executed along with Kosynka for alleged participation in a terrorist counter-revolutionary organization was Oleksa Vlyzko (1908–34). This young poet's collections were *Za vsikh skazhu* (I Will Tell for All, 1927) and *Zhyvu, pratsiuiu* (I Live, I Work, 1930). 'Vlyzko is one of the few representatives of revolutionary optimism. This optimism is natural to the poet, but so far appears rather superficial. It must be made more profound and philosophically well grounded to avoid the trivial. The author must seriously think about having close contact with revolutionary society and acquiring the psychology of the proletarian class in order to enrich his work thematically and avoid abstraction.'[48]

Another writer, Dmytro Falkivsky (1898–1934), was executed at the same time as Kosynka and Vlyzko. He was the author of the poem *Chaban* (Shepherd, 1925) and the collections *Obrii* (Horizons, 1927), *Na pozharyshchi* (After the Fire, 1928), and *Polissia* (1931). Iakiv Savchenko wrote that Falkivsky 'was enchanted by the cold reflection of the old, dying days.'[49] More recently, his poetry has again been criticized: 'The leading motif of Falkivsky's work, especially the poems included in the collection *After the Fire*, is the conflict between the interests of the individual and those of society, and doubts about the revolutionary struggle, which demands the sacrifice of the unique human life. Falkivsky's lyrical hero is not the builder of new life, but a dejected and passive man, a sacrifice for a distant goal.'[50]

The fourth writer to be executed in 1934 was Kost Burevii (1888–1934). He wrote a long story, *Khamy* (Boors, 1925); a book of essays, *Evropa chy Rosiia* (Europe or Russia, 1925); a verse parody, *Zozendropiia* (1928), under the pseudonym Edvard Strikha; and a comedy, *Chotyry Chemberleny* (Four Chamberlains, 1931). His play *Pavlo Polubotok*, written 'for the drawer,' was published in the West in 1955. Burevii was most talented as a parodist. 'Zozendropiia was a slap in the face not only to futurism, but to the entire 'proletarian' literature. It mercilessly revealed the vulgar and primitive essence of this literature, its helplessness, clumsiness, and slavish dependence on political programs. In fact, Eduard Strikha's mask was twofold. He donned the mask of a futurist in order to parody futurism, but the very parody of futurism was a mask to ridicule all genuine Soviet literature and, through it, the Soviet regime.'[51]

Another group of writers virtually annihilated in the purges was Zakhidnia Ukraina (Western Ukraine), consisting of immigrants from western parts of Ukraine (what was then Poland and Romania). Among them was a talented prose writer, Volodymyr Gzhytsky (1895–1973), author of the controversial novel *Chorne ozero* (The Black Lake, 1929). The novel, set in the Altai autonomous region, explored the behaviour of Russians and Ukrainians among the natives of Altai. The heroine, Tania, 'tries to defend her indeterminate position; she still has an incorrect understanding of patriotism and local exclusiveness. It seems to be that complete isolation will save the little people from haemorrhage.'[52] The author was severely chastised for his 'incorrect view.' In his work, to use the official phrase, 'there came a long pause (*nastupyla tryvala pauza*)'[53] In reality, Gzhytsky ended up in the Gulag, survived, and rewrote *The Black Lake* to the Party's liking.

Another immigrant from the west who shared Gzhytsky's fate was Dmytro Zahul (1890–1938), a native of Bukovina. His collections of poetry were *Z zelenykh hir* (From the Green Mountains, 1918), *Nash den* (Our Day, 1923), and *Motyvy* (Motifs, 1927). He also translated Goethe and Heine. Critics regarded him as a symbolist. 'Behind his new pose of life's realist there lurks the old shadow of the incorrigible idealist. In his new songs, glorifying the birth of the new, there are heard notes of spiritual anguish and sorrow.'[54]

Vasyl Bobynsky (1898–1938) was a native of Western Ukraine who, during the revolution, fought in the ranks of the nationalist Sich Sharpshooters and later became a staunch Communist. His early poetry collections *Nich kokhannia* (Night of Love, 1923) and *Taina tantsiu* (Mystery of Dance, 1924) 'displayed narrow, personal motifs ... from which minor melodies are heard.'[55] Bobynsky wrote a long poem, *Smert Franka* (Franko's Death, 1926), and many propagandist verses. These did not save him from the Gulag.

Another Western Ukrainian, who shared Bobynsky's fate, was Myroslav Irchan (1897–1937), a prolific playwright and prose writer. Among

his works are *Rodyna shchitkariv* (The Family of Brush-makers, 1923),
Bila malpa (The White Monkey, 1928), *Z prerii Kanady v stepy Ukrainy*
(From Canadian Prairies to Ukrainian Steppes, 1930), and *Platsdarm*
(Place d'Armes, 1933). He lived for some time in Canada. He was regarded as 'the most productive of the writers beyond the ocean, known
through his stories and plays, sometimes perhaps overextended, but
on the whole dynamic.'[56]

A very different writer, in temperament and conviction, was Mykhailo Ivchenko (1890–1939), the author of some short stories collected
in *Imlystoiu rikoiu* (Along a Misty River, 1926), and of the novel *Robitni
syly* (Working Forces, 1930). He was once called a 'pantheistic lyricist.'[57]
According to Oleksander Biletsky, 'a lyrical devotion to the soil and
complete union with it – this lyricism is the main charm of Ivchenko's
stories. There would be very little without it. Plot does not interest
him. There is no variety of characters or depth of observation in his
final works. In the end, they are also lacking in thought. The revolution
has left some trace, but the author has not experienced it deeply.'[58]
Working Forces got Ivchenko into trouble; he was arrested and perished
in a concentration camp.

A different spirit pervades the prose works of Andrii Holovko
(1897–1972). 'The images of Holovko's works, their life-confirming optimism, their cheerfulness and joy of victory inspire the reader with
such energy and joy of life, call him to move "forward and upward,"
to fight and to win, to embody in practice the best ideal of mankind
– Communism.'[59] Holovko's novel *Burian* (Weeds, 1927) was directed
against the *kulaks* and earned much praise. Few knew that it was heavily censored. 'The novel also had great educational and cognitive value
for the countries of the people's democracies that, using the experience
of the Soviet Union, are marching towards socialism.'[60] In 1932 Holovko
published a novel *Maty* (Mother), which he was forced to rewrite in
1935, emulating Gorky's novel of the same title. The path towards
'socialist realism' was secure.

A gifted poet who followed his own direction and tried to lead the
Avangard (avant-garde) group was Valeriian Polishchuk (1897–1942).
He was strongly influenced by Walt Whitman. Some of his many col-
lections of poems are *Vybukhy syly* (Explosions of Force, 1921), *Radio v
zhytakh* (Radio in the Ryefields, 1923), *Divchyna* (A Girl, 1925), and
Hryhorii Skovoroda (1929). 'Valeriian Polishchuk could do much more

than he already has, with his drive forward, eternal searchings, self-education, and following contemporary Western European as well as Eastern literature. His desire to create something new, to illumine a path into the future as well as to beautify the present, will last for a long time.'[61] Too individualistic for the tastes of the Party, Polishchuk was arrested and died in the Gulag. Some of his poems were republished after his rehabilitation.

Two writers of humorous prose did not escape arrest and incarceration. One of them, Ostap Vyshnia (1889–1956), was the most popular writer of the day, the author of several volumes of *Vyshnevi usmishky* (Vyshnia's Smiles, 1925–7). While most of his humour is drawn from the life of the peasants and the proletariat, some is directed against the bureaucracy and occasionally against himself ('Autobiography'). He returned from the Gulag in the 1950s and continued writing. Iurii Vukhnal (1906–37) was another humorist, who wrote *Zhyttia i diialnist Fedka Husky* (The Life and Activity of Fedko Huska, 1929). He perished in a concentration camp, but his works have since been republished.

In a genre not too far removed from that of Vyshnia and Vukhnal are the works of Serhii Pylypenko (1891–1943): *Baikivnytsia* (Book of Fables, 1922) and *Baiky* (Fables, 1927). 'In his fables, Pylypenko shows a double aim. First of all, this is an attempt to introduce a new kind of folk-story (the plots of the *Book of Fables* have nothing in common with Aesop's traditional fables), and secondly, this is the first attempt in the Ukrainian language to organize proletarian consciousness through a fable.'[62] Pylypenko will mostly be remembered as the founder and leader of the organization of peasant writers Pluh (The Plough). Along with many other members of the group he was arrested and died in internal exile.

Ideologically very different was the poet Mykola Tereshchenko (1898–1966), whose greatest contribution was made in the field of translation (Verhaeren). His early love of futurism was short-lived, and he became a Communist true believer as early as the 1920s.

The urban motifs in the poet's works were very prominent and led to the glorification of technology, the machine, and not of the people who created and directed it. This, of course, was borrowed from the futurists, with whom Tereshchenko had creative contacts in the 1920s. Yet even then the revolutionary principle was decisive in the poet's creativity. A correct understanding of the general development of Soviet society, outlined by the Communist Party, made it possible for Tereshchenko to join the ranks of the builders of socialism, Soviet culture and literature.[63]

Two playwrights deserve to be mentioned. Iakiv Mamontov (1888–1940) was the author of two popular plays: *Respublika na kolesakh* (A Republic on Wheels, 1928) and *Rozheve pavutynnia* (Pink Cobwebs, 1928). The former 'was a sharp, devastating satire on various puppet anti-democratic "governments" that, during the period of civil war, the international interventionist band of imperialists and the internal bourgeois-nationalist, Makhnovite-anarchist, and other counter-revolutions tried to foist upon the working masses of Ukraine.'[64] This and many other propagandist plays by Mamontov did not secure his future. He was purged, but rehabilitated in the 1950s.

Ivan Kocherha (1881–1952) was a very different dramatist, who at first wrote in Russian. He was the author of the plays *Feia hirkoho mihdalu* (The Bitter Almond Fairy, 1926), *Marko v pekli* (Marco in Hell, 1930), and *Pisnia pro Svichku* (Song about Svichka, 1931). The first of these was, in the opinion of the critics, 'not interesting because of its social ideas and tendencies, which are marginal and not organic to the work, but because of the masterfully drawn ancient customs and the humorous interchanges in various situations.'[65] In the late 1920s, in response to Party demands, he wrote a series of 'agitka' plays, which 'were neither true to life nor character.'[66] These 'schematic' works may have saved his life. His unquestioned talent appeared later.

A dramatist who, more than Kocherha, reflected the requirements of the Party, was Ivan Mykytenko (1897–1937). He wrote some prose and the plays *Dyktatura* (Dictatorship, 1929), *Kadry* (The Cadres, 1930), and *Divchata nashoi krainy* (Women of Our Land, 1932). 'The main idea of *Dictatorship*,' a critic wrote, 'is the struggle of the Communist Party and the Soviet state to strengthen the friendship between the working class and the working peasantry, a friendship that is the life-giving basis of the dictatorship of the proletariat.'[67] *The Cadres*, on the other hand, was a play about the struggle for the new higher education in the 'period of reconstruction.' These works, written in response to the first five-year plan propaganda, did not prevent a tragic denouement. Mykytenko allegedly shot himself before he could be arrested in 1937.

Another surprising victim of the purges was the dedicated Communist writer, Ivan Kulyk (1897–1941), who for some time in the 1920s served as a Soviet consul in Canada. He is best remembered as a translator of Walt Whitman and Carl Sandburg and as the editor of an anthology of American poetry (1928). He wrote a long poem, *Chorna epopeia* (Black Epic, 1929), about the blacks in the United States.

A much more talented poet and translator, Vasyl Mysyk (1907–83), was also a victim of the Gulag. He was the author of the collections *Travy* (Grasses, 1927), *Blakytny mist* (The Blue Bridge, 1929), and *Chotyry vitry* (Four Winds, 1930). After his release from the camp he was rehabilitated and his works republished.

Borys Teneta (1903–35) was a promising young prose writer, the author of a collection of short stories, *Lysty z Krymu* (Letters from the Crimea, 1927), and the novels *Harmoniia i svynushnyk* (Accordion and Pigsty, 1928) and *Nenavyst* (Hatred, 1930). He committed suicide during a police interrogation. A poet whose talent remained unfulfilled was Leonid Chernov (1899–1933). His short stories are collected in *Sontse pid veslamy* (Sun under the Oars, 1927) and his poems in *Na rozi bur* (Crossing the Storm, 1934). As a young man he travelled to China and India. He was one of the few writers of some originality to die a natural death.

The poet Andrii Paniv (1899–1937), one of the founders of Pluh, was the author of a collection, *Vechirni tini* (Evening Shadows, 1927). Like many of the lesser lights of the 'peasant' writers, he ended his days in a concentration camp. He was rehabilitated in 1960. His fate was shared by Oleksander Sokolovsky (1896–1938). Sokolovsky's historical novel *Bohun* (1931) was described as 'nationalist contraband.'[68]

A mammoth novel about changing conditions in Soviet central Asia, *Roman Mizhhiria* (The Novel of Mizhhiria, 1929) was written by Ivan Le (1895–1978). The second part of the novel appeared five years later, after the author took the advice of his critics to transform his hero. Later Le excelled in the genre of historical fiction.

One of the 'peasant' poets with a Komsomol mentality was Pavlo Usenko (1902–75). His poems were collected in *KSM* (1925) and *Poezii* (Poems, 1932). Occasionally he showed some lyrical talent.

The relative liberalism of the 1920s came to an end at the close of the decade. The political events heralding the change were the ending of the NEP in 1928 and the initiation, in the same year, of the first five year plan – preliminaries to the consolidation of absolute power in the hands of Joseph Stalin. The policy of 'Ukrainization' was soft-pedalled and eventually abandoned.

These developments signalled the tightening of Party controls not only over the economy, but over cultural life as well. The forced mobilization of all human resources for the carrying out of the first five year plan had a most direct influence on literature. Thematically and stylistically it was propelled, by ceaseless exhortation and criticism, towards the goals of Communist propaganda. What in the 1920s was the prerogative of Communist writers alone now became the universal yardstick of literary creation. No exceptions were tolerated.

Literary life in the 1920s revolved around several literary groups and organizations – Pluh, Hart, VAPLITE, Lanka, the neoclassicists, the futurists, the constructivists, etc. This variety brought about lively controversies and polemics and allowed for a certain cultural pluralism, which was never to be tolerated later. An event extraordinary in itself was the 'literary discussion' (1925–8), the last free debate on cultural and political issues in Ukraine. Various cultural and aesthetic theories were represented, and the result was that Ukraine, although Communist, came to have a high culture of its own. But gradual pressure from the Party, often combined with police interference, led to the dissolution of some groups in the late 1920s and the creation of VUSPP, Vseukrainska spilka proletarskykh pysmennykiv (All-Ukrainian Alliance of Proletarian Writers), as the Party's watchdog over literature. Then suddenly, in April 1932, by Party decree, all the remaining literary groups were dissolved to prepare the way for the creation of the All-Union Writers' Union, in which national bodies were to become mere branches of the new literary bureaucracy centred in Moscow.

These transformations, entirely forced from above, coincided with the beginning of the arrests of writers that later, in Ukraine, became a wholesale purge. Of the fifty-seven writers discussed in this chapter, thirty-six, or almost two-thirds, perished in the Gulag. This pogrom had catastrophic effects on literature. In the 1920s the various genres had developed their own practitioners, who followed different models and practices. The most varied field was that of poetry where such different talents as Bazhan, Pluzhnyk, Rylsky, Svidzinsky, Tychyna, and Zerov forcefully enlarged the horizons of Ukrainian poetry. In prose, too, the first-rate talents of Ianovsky, Iohansen, Khvylovy, Kosynka, Pidmohylny, and others showed great promise. In drama Kulish and Kurbas were of world stature. The modernist impulse of innovation and experimentation was alive and well. The entire era was a time when literature in Ukraine came closest to its European pluralistic patrimony. One can and should study it in that context. The literary criticism of the decade produced some striking achievements in, for example, the work of Biletsky, Doroshkevych, Iakubsky, Koriak, and Zerov. They were gradually supplanted by official critics whose methods were more akin to police denunciation. A stern new muse was showing its face – the face of a policeman.

3 The Trauma of Socialist Realism 1934–53

It took more than two years, from April 1932 to August 1934, to prepare for the formation of the Writers' Union, at the First congress of Soviet Writers in Moscow. The delay was partly due to some passive resistance on the part of reluctant writers, but also to a new constellation of political power, with Stalin emerging after the Party Congress in 1932 as the undisputed leader. The first five-year plan was declared completed ahead of schedule in 1932 (fraudulently, as we now know), and the stage was set for the 'building of socialism in one country.' The opposition within Party ranks and within the peasantry had been crushed, and the intellectuals, who had been banished to the Gulag, provided ample warning to their colleagues that the Party would tolerate no wavering. As Petro Panch said during the Moscow congress, 'the victory looks significant only when it is achieved by conquering the obstacles.'[1]

In Ukraine, the obstacles were often writers themselves, who had to be 'liquidated.' The purges referred to in chapter 2 reached much greater proportions as the 1930s progressed. A study by me[2] of the human losses estimated that 254 writers perished in the thirties as a result of police repression. More recent figures, provided by a Russian researcher in 1988, put the toll of all Ukrainian writers 'liquidated' in the 1930s at 500,[3] half the total of all Soviet writers who perished at that time. This literary bloodbath was accompanied by purges of Ukrainian scholars, teachers, and clergymen. At about the same time, especially in 1932–3, the man-made famine during the forced collectivization in Ukraine swept away nearly seven million peasants.[4] A few years later, the

Communist Party of Ukraine was decimated and the entire government of the country incarcerated.

Traumas such as these were devastating, yet not a word was printed about these tragedies. The destruction of the entire country was re-ceived·either with silence or with renewed calls to build Communism. Only in 1988, during the era of *glasnost*, was the fate of literature in the 1930s admitted:

The sad statistics of one Muscovite literary enthusiast [E. Beltov] became known: from 1000 cards that he made out for writers (not only members of the Writers' Union) who were victims of repression, almost half were those who wrote in our republic. So did Stalin's and Kaganovich's heroes trample our literature. Let us add to this martyrology a great number of writers (sometimes of great stature) who violated their own talents to fit in with Stalinist ideology and also those who remained honest only by twisting their creations and whittling them in half, and the conclusion is obvious: during the ill-fated personality cult there was a pogrom of Ukrainian literature as such ...[5]

Speaking in 1988, Borys Oliinyk declared that 'the fact [is] that if not four out of five then literally two out of three Ukrainian writers were either shot, or driven into Stalin's camps, from which only a few re-turned.'[6]

Much remains to be discovered about the details of the purges. Why, for instance, did they include some faithful Communists and Party hacks such as Kulyk and Mykytenko? For the time being, perhaps Arthur Koestler's dictum about the 'purge of the purgers' may explain this. Some critics in the West – for example, Shevelov – suggested that the purges were directed primarily against those writers who used universal themes in their works[7] and that they were an attempt to force narrow, ethnic parameters. There is some truth in this, but it is also true that hundreds of those 'liquidated' did not have universal preten-sions.

Were there any protests against this bloodbath? The most telling was the suicide of Mykola Khvylovy in May 1933, followed a few months later by the suicide of Mykola Skrypnyk, an old Bolshevik and at the time the commissar of education in Ukraine. In 1937 Panas Liubchenko, the head of the Soviet Ukrainian government, also committed suicide before his expected arrest. There were other writers who took their own lives rather than face the purges. Other forms of protest were impossible under the existing police terror. Some writers – Khvylovy in his short stories, Zerov and Pluzhnyk in their poetry, Dniprovsky in his letters – expressed dark forebodings about the future. But the general silence on the one hand and the congratulatory salvos of Party propaganda about the destruction of the 'enemies of the people' on the other, amounted almost to obscenity.

The Writers' Congress in Moscow in 1934 approved the statute of the new Writers' Union with its rights and obligations. The executive bodies of the Union became a part of the *nomenklatura* with all the residual duties and benefits. The Soviet intelligentsia became the handmaiden of the Party. Ideologically, a new theory or 'method' of 'socialist realism' was proclaimed as binding on all writers. According to this theory, literary works had 'to reflect reality in its revolutionary development' and 'educate readers in the spirit of socialism.[8] Maksim Gorky, known for his insulting remarks about Ukrainians (in a letter to Ukrainian writers he referred to their language as a 'dialect'), was enthroned as the patron saint of the new Soviet literature. A long period of sustained control of literature by the Party followed, which, with some minor exceptions during The Second World War, lasted till Stalin's death in 1953.

The pluralistic, liberal atmosphere of the 1920s was constantly permeated by calls to build a new proletarian revolution, dedicated to the ideals of communism. Some writers did not heed these calls and continued their own work, but many listened with attention to the proclamation of a new era. There was some scepticism, but there was also a great deal of idealism. All the writers paid lip service to the revolution, and many hoped that new policies would lead to greater human happiness. It is therefore impossible to dissect the souls of writers caught in a terrible dilemma in the thirties, when it was made perfectly clear that the time for vacillation was over and that their works must from then on be totally dedicated to 'the people,' that is, to the Party, which allegedly represented the people's interests. There are indications that those who escaped the purges did find it difficult to embrace 'socialist realism' at first, but that gradually they all willingly supported it. Self-censorship became the practice of the day.

Of paramount importance here is the case of Pavlo Tychyna, some of whose early works, especially *Instead of Sonnets and Octaves* (1920), were frowned upon. A short collection of his verse, *Chernihiv* (1931), may be viewed as a transition from the early, lyrical Tychyna to the later glorifier of Stalin. G. Grabowicz, discussing the genre of the collection, states: 'It seems clear that it is not reportage, nor even so much a veristic dramatic portrait, as it is a vision, a distillation of the popular Ukraine in transition, presented through the verbal analogue of a musical composition – not a 'symphony' like *Skovoroda*, but a cantata. It is a polyphony of voices and rhythms and moods, captured with manifold artistry and subtly modulated control. It is yet another instance of Tychyna's restless creativity discovering new forms.'[9]

By 1934, Tychyna was ready to turn a new leaf with the publication of a collection entitled *Partiia vede* (The Party Leads). The chief poem of this collection, with the same title, was printed in Ukrainian in *Pravda* in 1933. There followed *Chuttia iedynoi rodyny* (The Feeling of a United Family, 1938), *Stal i nizhnist* (Steel and Tenderness, 1941), and many propagandist verses written during and after the war. 'The central theme of [Tychyna's] poetic works during the war,' writes a critic, 'was the theme of the socialist fatherland. The native land, in Tychyna's verses, is painted at a moment of mortal danger as a picture of a proud and invincible mother.'[10] At the time of the battle of Stalingrad Tychyna wrote a long and beautiful elegy, 'Pokhoron druha' (The Burial of a Friend, 1943). Between 1920 and 1940 he laboured on a long poem, *Skovoroda*, which, according to an émigré critic, has anti-Stalinist overtones.[11] For his loyalty Tychyna was rewarded with medals and high official posts; he was for a while the minister of education in Soviet Ukraine. A significant commentary on Tychyna under Stalin appeared in Soviet Ukraine in 1988: 'Writers and artists such as Tychyna, Rylsky, Bazhan, Sosiura and others experienced moral torture and were forced to write "Long live Stalin" ... We are talking about the "barrack socialism" of the 1930s. Barracks are for the army and an army has to take a loyalty oath. Writers also had to take such an oath, every book began with such an oath ... It must be said that Pavlo Tychyna's verses written to support and propagate the official course were strangely weak and sometimes almost parodies.'[12] Attempts to maintain that Tychyna, under Stalin, remained true to his poetic form, seem spurious.

Maksym Rylsky was another prominent poet who after 1930 placed himself at the service of the Party. In that year he wrote a poem, first published in 1965, in which he admitted that, for a brief time, he had been arrested and spent time at the house of Compulsory Labour (BUPR).[13] This experience had the intended effect, and in 1932 Rylsky published a collection, *Znak tereziv* (The Sign of Libra), which began with the poem 'A Declaration of the Duties of the Poet and the Citizen.' The collection 'bore witness to the decisive turnaround in the poet's consciousness during the years of the first five-year plan, his desire to become a builder and singer of the classless socialist society.'[14] There followed the collections *Kyiv* (Kiev, 1935), *Lito* (Summer, 1936), and *Zbir vynohradu* (Gathering of Grapes, 1940), all 'permeated with a gay, optimistic view of life, a passionate love for contemporary life, for the people and its leader – the Communist Party.'[15] During the war, apart from Soviet patriotic verse, Rylsky wrote a good long poem, *Zhaha* (Yearning, 1943), dedicated to his native land, which drew a great deal of official criticism. Critics were not pleased with the collection *Mandrivka v molodist* (Travel into My Youth, 1944), either, and the poet had to rewrite it. He returned to stark Communist propaganda in *Mosty* (Bridges, 1948), only to revert after Stalin's death to the early lyricism in his collection *Holosiivska osin* (The Autumn of Holosiiv, 1959).

Volodymyr Sosiura overcame his waverings and became a Party stalwart. We know now that in 1929 he started to write 'for the drawer' a novel, *Tretia rota* (the name of his native village), which was first published in 1988. It expressed his frustrations, disappointments, and anger with the regime. On the surface, however, Sosiura remained a 'socialist realist.' In 1932 he published the collection *Vidpovid* (The Answer), which included the poem 'Dniprelstan' (The Dnieper Dam, first written in 1926). In this volume he lashed out, as he used to do in the 1920s, against Ukrainian 'bourgeois nationalists,' especially Dmytro Dontsov and Ievhen Malaniuk in Polish Ukraine. During 1933 and 1934 the poet did not publish a 'single book of poems and was rarely printed in the periodical press.'[16] In 1940 he published a long autobiographical poem, *Chervonohvardiets* (Red Guardsman). Near the end of the war he wrote a short poem, 'Liubit Ukrainu' (Love Ukraine, 1944), which a few years later was sharply attacked as 'nationalist.' This, once more, produced in Sosiura a sobering effect, and a decade later he wrote: 'The Party has taught me to understand life as an eternal creation, an endless movement towards the new and the better ... It gives us unbreakable wings, magnificent wings to soar aloft. To serve people as a Communist is the greatest happiness on earth.'[17]

The fourth major poet who was untouched by the purges was Mykola Bazhan. In 1932 he wrote a poem, 'Smert Hamleta' (Hamlet's Death), containing these lines: 'The only great and true humanity / Is the Leninist class-warfare humanity.'[18] Always given to philosophical poetry, he now embraced Marxism-Leninism-Stalinism. Leonid Novychenko sums up this conversion: 'Chaos was always hateful for Bazhan, particularly the chaos of confusion and despair. "The will fixes the decision, form rises out of chaos." And so his Communist builder enters the ruins and the image of this poem becomes the symbolic picture of the new day.'[19] In 1935–7 Bazhan wrote a long poem, *Bezsmertia* (Immortality), about Kirov. It ends with the lines: 'Live, immortal life, / The life of the bolsheviks!'[20]

During the war Bazhan wrote *Stalinhradsky zoshyt* (The Stalingrad Notebook, 1943) and *Kyivski etiudy* (The Kiev Etudes, 1945). After the war he travelled to England and Italy and left some very questionable poetic impressions of both countries. Not until the 1960s did he return to his earlier muse.

Iurii Ianovsky's prose was often criticized in the 1920s for its romanticism. Now, having placed himself at the disposal of the regime, he used his earlier technique to write ideologically more appropriate works. In 1935 he published *Vershnyky* (Riders), a novel curiously reminiscent in both structure and tone of the earlier *Four Sabres*.

In style, imagery, and general structure the author achieved unity between the legend and concrete historical reality, between the social psychology of the era and the precision of ideological evaluation. The military and historical panorama in this condensed heroic epic is much wider than in the *Four Sabres*. There are the battles between the partisan units and the red detachments, episodes of underground work in enemy camp, strategic leadership by the Party of the working masses, while among the heroes there are not only those created by the author's imagination, but also historic personages, well-known revolutionaries, and prominent military leaders.[21]

In 1957, with the title *Les Cavaliers*, the novel appeared in French translation with a glowing preface by Louis Aragon.

Ianovsky's play *Duma pro Brytanku* (A Duma about Brytanka) was published in Russian in 1937 and in Ukrainian a year later. It dealt with the revolution and the civil war. After the war, Ianovsky's novel *Zhyva voda* (Living Waters, 1947) was severely criticized; it reappeared in radically revised form, entitled *Myr* (Peace), after the author's death. Also first in Russian, Ianovsky's play *Dochka prokurora* (The Procurator's Daughter) was performed in 1954, a week before his death.

Petro Panch continued writing propagandist prose. In the novel *Obloha nochi* (The Siege of Night, 1932–5) he returned to the theme of civil war. 'Using his artistic experience from his earlier antibourgeois stories in the collection *The Blue Echelons*, particularly the unmasking of the negative characters, Panch depicts the multifaceted counter-revolutionary camp, all sorts of monarchists, bourgeois nationalists, anarchists, Mensheviks, all united by a fear of revolution, or simply opportunists and cowards who would rather wait and see what happens ...'[22]

After the war Panch wrote a historical novel *Homonila Ukraina* (Ukraine Was Humming, 1958) about Bohdan Khmelnytsky and Maksym Kryvonis. 'The Marxist-Leninist understanding of phenomena and social processes helped the author to depict correctly the class stratification among the Poles and Ukrainians and subtly stress the social and class elements in popular mass movement. Many striking episodes and portraits, as well as characters, convincingly confirm the belief about the age-long relationship between the Ukrainian and Russian peoples and show how the idea of the re-unification of the two brotherly peoples was born among the masses.'[23]

Three prose writers left unscathed by the purges were Smolych, Kopylenko, and Holovko, who continued their activity in the 1930s and 1940s. Smolych lampooned the 'bourgeois nationalists' in *Po toi bik sertsia* (On This Side of the Heart, 1930) and derided capitalism in *Sorok visim hodyn* (Forty-Eight Hours, 1933). *Shcho bulo potim* (What Happened Later, 1934) is propagandist science fiction. His autobiographical trilogy – *Dytynstvo* (Childhood, 1937), *Nashi tainy* (Our Secrets, 1936), and *Visimnadtsiatylitni* (The Eighteen-Year-Old, 1938) – was very popular, as was the autobiographical *Teatr nevidomoho aktora* (The Theater of the Unknown Actor, 1940). During and after the war Smolych was a prolific journalist, expressing his venom for the nationalists. In 1953 he published an epic novel about the civil war in 1919, *Svitanok nad morem* (Dawn over the Sea). He continued writing until his death (see page 69).

Oleksander Kopylenko wrote his novel *Narodzhuietsia misto* (A City Is Born) about the 'socialist construction' in 1931–2. He also wrote novels for young people, one of which was *Duzhe dobre* (Very Good, 1936). He did not distinguish himself as a writer either during or after the war.

Andrii Holovko worked a long time on his novel *Artem Harmash* (1951–60), about the perennial topic of the struggle between the Communists and nationalists during the revolution. The evil spirit of nationalism had to be exorcised forever.

Mykola Tereshchenko published several collections of poetry during the war, among them *Vinok slavy* (The Wreath of Glory 1942). He continued writing sonnets and translating.

In 1933 Ivan Kocherha's philosophical play *Maistry chasu* (Masters of Time) was quite successful. His *Vybir* (The Choice, 1938) is a play on a topical issue of 1937, suspicion of treason. Its first performance was in Moscow in 1939, but afterwards the play was banned. It was not until 1944, under the impact of the war, that he wrote his greatest play, *Iaroslav Mudry*, born 'of a sharp feeling of the greatness of national traditions ... when his patriotism and national feeling became weightier in his creative life.'[24]

Ivan Le continued writing about village life in a novel about the new Soviet woman, *Istoriia radosti* (The Story of Joy, 1938). In 1940 he published a historical novel, *Nalyvaiko*. Le found a 'positive hero' in sixteenth-century Ukraine. This led him to write a trilogy, *Khmelnytsky* (1939–64), which completed his career.

The optimistic lyricism of Pavlo Usenko found expression throughout the 1930s to the 1950s. His poetry collections were *Liryka boiu* (The Lyrics of Struggle, 1934), *Poezii* (Poems, 1937), *Za Ukrainu* (For Ukraine, 1941), and *Dorohamy iunosty* (Along the Paths of Youth, 1950).

Apart from those writers who began their careers in the 1920s, many new faces entered the literary scene as Party controls were tightening, and distinguished themselves during the period of 'socialist realism.' They were often valued not so much for their talent as for their devotion to the Party. The most prominent of them, who became the leading playwright of the era as well as the commanding *apparatchik* of the Ukrainian branch of the Writers' Union, was Oleksander Korniichuk

(1905–72). His first play, *Na hrani* (On Edge, 1928), showed his interest in the problems of the Soviet 'creative intelligentsia,' a subject to which he later returned. Fame came to him with his plays *Zahybel eskadry* (Death of a Naval Squadron) and *Platon Krechet*, both appearing in 1934. While the former deals with the revolution and the civil war, the latter, in his own words, 'demonstrated the rapture of human thought, free from mysticism and idealism, in the struggle for a new life.'[25] The surgeon Platon Krechet is the embodiment of the new Soviet superman, the apogee of 'sunny optimism, humanism, and patriotism.' In 1938 Korniichuk wrote the play *Bohdan Khmelnytsky*. The hero, 'a brave and courageous man, well educated and a good diplomat, has met the expectations of his era, the longing of the people, and the thoughts and hopes of the working masses. The greatest human and states-manlike achievement of Bohdan Khmelnytsky was the Pereiaslav Council (1654), which proclaimed the re-unification of Ukraine with Russia.'[26]

During the war Korniichuk wrote a topical propaganda play, *Front* (Front, 1942), excerpts from which appeared in *Pravda*. In 1945 he wrote his 'American' play, *Misiia mistera Perkinsa v krainu bilshovykiv* (The Mission of Mr Perkins into the Land of the Bolsheviks). The first signs of the post-Stalin 'thaw' are clearly seen in Korniichuk's *Kryla* (The Wings, 1954), showing the old opportunist at his best. As the secretary of the Ukrainian branch of the Writers' Union for more than fifteen years, he dominated literary life and was richly rewarded with medals and honours.

A much more talented writer, of Jewish descent, was Leonid Per-vomaisky (1908–73), who was primarily a poet but who also wrote prose and plays. As a young member of the Komsomol he produced two collections of poetry, *Nova liryka* (New Lyrics, 1934–7) and *Barvinkovy svit* (The Periwinkle World, 1937–9). 'Pervomaisky's poetry grew or-ganically from the idea of the "unique and immortal" time of the first five-year plans, the industrialization period, and the collectivization of agriculture, and therefore one can sense in it the aroma of the times, the rhythm of the epoch, the rhythm of work, of storm brigades in factories and collective farms, the pathos of the tempos. The poet's works are permeated by joy in the people's achievements in economic and cultural construction.'[27] The true greatness of Pervomaisky was not fulfilled until after 1953.

Another Jewish writer, writing in Ukrainian, was Natan Rybak (1913–78), who became known chiefly for his two novels, *Pomylka Onore de Balzaka* (The Mistake of Honoré de Balzac, 1940) and *Pereiaslavska rada* (The Council of Pereiaslav, 1949–53). The former was based on Balzac's relationship with Evelyn Hanska, and 'truthfully depicts Balzac's errors and limitations. The author shows the power of money and Balzac's bourgeois enthusiasm for grandiose titles as well as his fruitless attempts to grow rich through speculation.'[28] The historical novel about Pereiaslav depicts 'the brave struggle of the Ukrainian people shoulder to shoulder with their Russian brethren against foreign exploiters.'[29] Even Soviet critics admitted that in doing this, 'Rybak solves the problem too simply, by forcing his heroes to deliver fierce tirades.'[30]

A writer who began his career in the 1920s and who wrote about the village and the city proletariat was Iakiv Kachura (1897–1943). He also wrote the historical novel *Ivan Bohun* (1940), which was 'the first attempt in a Ukrainian historical novel to reveal, from the position of Marxist-Leninist science, the profound content of the re-unification of Ukraine with Russia and its historic role in the lives of the two fraternal peoples.'[31]

An interest in history was also shown by Leonid Smiliansky (1904–66), the author of *Mykhailo Kotsiubynsky* (1940) and a play about Ivan Franko – *Muzhytsky posol* (The Peasant Deputy, 1945), and by Oleksander Ilchenko (b. 1909), the author of a novel about Shevchenko, *Sertse zhde* (The Heart Awaits, 1939). Ilchenko also later wrote the best seller *Kozatskomu rodu nema perevodu* (There Is No End to the Cossack Breed, 1944–57), the first Ukrainian 'whimsical' novel.

A writer of historical fiction who served some time in the Gulag, was Zinaida Tulub (1890–1964), the author of *Liudolovy* (Mencatchers, 1934), which she revised three times. She continued her career in the 1960s. Another inmate of the Gulag was Hordii Kotsiuba (1892–1939). After writing the novels *Novi berehy* (The New Shores, 1932) and *Rodiuchist* (Fertility, 1934), he disappeared from literary activity in the late 1930s. Iakiv Bash (1908–86) was the author of the popular war thriller *Profesor Buiko* (1946), which he later adapted into a play. Anatolii Shyian (1906–89) wrote the novel *Magistral* (1934) and many books for young readers. A writer who specialized almost entirely in the genre of juvenile literature was Oles Donchenko (1902–54). He produced more than 50 volumes. Kost Hordienko (b. 1899) was an orthodox prose writer, author of the novels *Dity zemli* (Children of the Earth, 1937) and *Chuzhu nyvu zhala* (She Moved a Foreign Meadow, 1940). Another 'socialist realist' of some repute was Oleksa Desniak (1909–42), the author of the novel *Desnu pereishly bataliony* (The Battalions Have Crossed the Desna, 1937).

Two prominent 'socialist realist' poets were Teren Masenko (1903–70) and Andrii Malyshko (1912–70). Masenko specialized in eulogizing the Soviet 'fraternal family of nations.' In 1937–8 he wrote a novel in verse, *Step* (Steppe). 'The author, with great warmth and love, speaks of the beauty of the southern steppe, of the pleasant if somewhat naive figures of working peasants, their lives and customs. The fresh, changing colours, laid on without sharp contrast, and the soft lyricism, pathos, and humour in the depiction of his native land are used in the creation of this poetic work.'[32]

A talented lyricist, who had to fight many battles with the censor, was Andrii Malyshko. His early collection of poems was *Batkivshchyna* (Native Land, 1936). 'Throughout all Malyshko's early works there appears the symbolic, generalized portrait of the land. The land, where a man was born, grew up, and learned to be happy. A free and joyful land, richly soaked with the blood of fathers and grandfathers. This land is the most beautiful, the richest, the most intimate in the world. The greatest happiness is to live on this native land, to enjoy its beauty and to make it more beautiful and wealthier. The rich, generous, free, and blooming land is a synonym for the Soviet fatherland ...'[33] Malyshko's long poem *Prometei* (Prometheus, 1946) was the 'synthesis of a new philosophy of life arising in a time of great trials [of war].'[34] In 1950 he published a collection of scurrilous verse about America, *Za synim morem* (Beyond the Blue Sea).

The period of the flowering of 'socialist realism' (1932–53) was sterile as far as literary accomplishment goes. At best, many of the prominent works, praising Stalin and the Party, could be classed as a new hagiography, reminiscent of the medieval lives of the saints. In the twentieth century this was an anachronism. Under Stalin's rule Soviet society was transformed, but not as the glowing literary works portrayed it to be – not towards greater humaneness and freedom. On the contrary, terror, coercion, and wholesale murder created, in the words of a Soviet writer in 1988, 'an atmosphere of fear among both old and young. This could be explained by repression, unjustified accusations of our nationalist writers, many court proceedings, silencing, and persecution.'[35]

Some slackening in the coercion occurred during the Second World
War. Many writers were forcibly evacuated as the Germans advanced,
but some managed to stay behind. Many joined the Red Army, and
in general, Ukrainian patriotism, although with a Soviet accent, was
encouraged in literature. Immediately after the war hopes were expressed for greater artistic freedom. These hopes were soon dashed,
however, when in 1946 Andrei Zhdanov delivered his attack on the
Russian journals *Zvezda* and *Leningrad*. In Ukraine, the Zhdanovist
period of repression (1946–53) was also widely felt. The need for *partiinost* (Party spirit) in literature was openly proclaimed and made compulsory. In 1951 Sosiura was severely attacked for the poem 'Liubit
Ukrainu' (Love Ukraine).

'Socialist realism' brought some new themes, favoured by the Party,
to Ukrainian literature. Among them was the obligatory subject of the
'friendship of Soviet peoples.' Works by Rylsky, Bazhan, Mysyk, and
Kulyk belong to this category. The revolutionary wars in Spain and
China found many literary exponents. Dmytro Bedzyk (1898–1982) wrote
what was expected of him, but it was not literature. Science fiction was
represented by Mykola Trublaini (1907–41) and Volodymyr Vladko
(1900–74). There was an immediate response to the Second World War
in the novels *Krov Ukrainy* (Ukraine's Blood, 1943) by Vadym Sobko
(1912–81) and *Praporonostsi* (Standard-bearers, 1946–8) by Oles Honchar
(b. 1918). The reconquest of the Western Ukrainian territories was portrayed in *Bukovynska povist* (Bukovinian Novel, 1951) by Ihor Muratov
(1912–73) and *Nad Cheremoshem* (Over the Cheremosh, 1952) by Mykhailo Stelmakh (1912–83). Yet most literary works kept to well-worn
'socialist realist' themes: socialist construction in the cities, collectivization in the villages, with those old stand-bys – the revolution and
civil war and the ever-present struggle against 'bourgeois nationalists.'
In all these works the positive hero shone – the 'new Soviet man,' a
Utopian creation if there ever was one. In the words of a prominent
émigré critic, 'from the perspective of the future, this twenty-year
period [1930–50] will yawn like a dead vacuum. Maybe a line or a stanza
here and there, or a paragraph of prose will be found, which will testify
to the tragedy of men conscious of their talent who were unable to
leave behind a whole work.'[36] Yet the enforced vision of revolution
and social progress under Communism could not be questioned.

4 The Thaw 1953-72

Immediately after Stalin's death in March 1953, 'socialist realism' was challenged in Russia. In Ukraine it took a little longer, but with Khrushchev's secret speech about Stalin's crimes at the Twentieth Party Congress in 1956, Ukrainian writers, too, began to deviate from the accepted norm.

In 1956, a lyrical autobiographical novel, *Zacharovana Desna* (The Enchanted Desna), was published by Oleksander Dovzhenko (1894–1956). Dovzhenko, an original member of VAPLITE in the 1920s, was a world-famous film producer. His film scenarios, some written in the 1920s, were reworked and first published as 'film-tales' in the 1950s: *Zemlia* (Earth, 1955), *Arsenal* (1957), *Shchors* (1957), *Povist polumianykh lit* (A Tale of the Fiery Years, 1957), and *Ukraina v ohni* (Ukraine in Flames, 1966). Dovzhenko lived in Moscow for many years, banned from Ukraine. His fascinating diary was published in censored form in the late 1950s, and not until 1988 were the deleted passages, critical of Stalin and Stalinism, made public. Maksym Rylsky wrote this about Dovzhenko's art: 'Oleksander Dovzhenko was a widely talented man, calling to mind the artists of the Renaissance era. His love of sharp tones and contrasts, of the visible world with its limitless play of colour and light and shadow, with its living beauty, made him akin to the artists of the Renaissance and to those of the Romantic era as well as to all those who glorify the abundance of life.'[1]

A prose writer who came to prominence under Stalin but became a leader in his field after Stalin's death as Mykhailo Stelmakh. His novel *Velyka ridnia* (A Great Family, 1951), full of praise for Stalin, was reworked into another novel, *Krov liudska ne vodytsia* (Human Blood Is

Not Water, 1957), where all the passages about Stalin were simply deleted. His other 'epic' works were *Khlib i sil* (Bread and Salt, 1959) and *Pravda i kryvda* (Truth and Injury, 1961). In the novel *Chotyry brody* (Four Fords, written and rewritten 1961–74), he attempted some mild criticism of Stalinism. Otherwise, his glorification of village life under Stalin's rule amounts, at best, to what Milan Kundera called 'political *kitsch*,' at worst, to an obscenity.

An older writer who finally came into his own after Stalin's death was Leonid Pervomaisky. His intimate, lyrical long poem *Kazka* (A Fable. 1958) was severely criticized. His best work, oddly enough in prose, is the novel *Dyky med* (Wild Honey, 1962).

This novel is without precedent in the entire canon of Ukrainian literature for its compositional structure. It deals with the difficult experience of Soviet men during the Iezhov era and during the Second World War up to today. The author refused to tell the story chronologically. He shifts events unexpectedly in time and space, using different devices: reminiscences, diaries, unexpected meetings, etc. ... Such a novel could only be written by someone who was thoroughly familiar with the contemporary European novel, particularly the French novel, which was strongly influenced by Marcel Proust. The dominant motif in Pervomaisky's novel is the Proustian search for 'lost time.'[2]

After Khrushchev's speech to the Twentieth Party Congress some of the writers who had perished in the purges were rehabilitated, and those who were still alive among them Vyshnia, Gzhytsky, Antonenko-Davydovych – were allowed to return home. The rehabilitation was very selective and incomplete. The republished works were inevitably 'selected,' and many prominent writers – for example, Khvylovy, Pidmohylny – were still proscribed. Yet the result of this partial vindication of Stalin's victims was incalculable. Some older writers from the first generation of Soviet Ukrainian literature became human once more and strayed a little beyond Party control. Unfortunately, the ever-cautious Tychyna was not among them. For him no return was possible to the earlier lyricism that had made him famous.

Two other doyens of literature, however, Rylsky and Bazhan, were capable of sensing and responding to the winds of change. Rylsky did this in a collection of verse, *Holosiivska osin* (The Autumn of Holosiiv, 1959), and even more openly in a series of articles, *Vechirni rozmovy*

(Evening Conversations, 1962), in which he welcomed the youngest generation of poets. Mykola Bazhan recaptured some of his early glory in *Chotyry opovidannia pro nadiiu, variatsii na temu R.M. Rilke* (Four Tales about Hope: Variations on a Theme by R.M. Rilke, 1966). Iurii Smolych, too, published several volumes of interesting and revealing memoirs about the 1920s: *Rozpovid pro nespokii* (The Tale about Restlessness, 1968), *Rozpovid pro nespokii tryvaie* (The Tale about Restlessness Continues, 1969) and *Rozpovidi pro nespokii nemaie kintsia* (The Tale about Restlessness Has No End, 1972). Smolych was reprimanded, however, for writing sympathetically about the 'odious' personalities of the 1920s.

Several writers turned to historical themes, dealing with them less dogmatically than in the previous years. Among them was Semen Skliarenko (1901–62), author of *Sviatoslav* (1959) and *Volodymyr* (1962), and Pavlo Zahrebelny (b. 1924), the author of *Dyvo* (A Marvel, 1968). Zinaida Tulub published a novel about Shevchenko's years in exile, *V stepu bezkraim za Uralom* (Amid the Limitless Steppes Beyond the Urals, 1964). Hryhorii Tiutiunnyk (1920–61) avoided the clichés of 'socialist realism' in his novel about a collective farm, *Vyr* (Whirlpool, 1959–61). In the 1960s Vasyl Kozachenko (b. 1913) wrote a novel, *Koni voronii* (Raven Black Horses), in which he devoted a chapter to the famine of 1933. The novel remained unpublished until 1988.

Oles Honchar was born in 1918 and belongs to the recent generation of writers, although he was first published in 1938. His reputation as a fine prose writer was established by the trilogy *Praporonostsi* (Standard-bearers, 1946–8). His celebrated novel *Liudyna i zbroia* (Man and Arms, 1959) is described in a history of Soviet Ukrainian literature as follows:

Many novels about war have appeared in world literature during the last few decades. Man is depicted in many of these foreign works as a helpless, beaten creature. The hard life in the trenches, constant danger, the horror of war quickly destroy people, deaden their feelings, limit their interests. Recall, for example, Richard Aldington's novel *Death of a Hero* or Remarque's *All Quiet on the Western Front*. In Honchar's novels as in all Soviet literature dedicated to war themes, the horrors of war and its evil are contrasted with the invincible force of humanity, encouraged in our citizens by the socialist way of life.[3]

Honchar's *Sobor* (The Cathedral, 1968) is a very different novel. At first it was favourably received, then violently attacked and banned, only to be republished in 1988. Honchar, a veteran 'socialist realist,' had committed the unpardonable sin of fanning nationalist passions. The novel, which is inferior in style, centres on the problem of a sense of historical awareness among some Soviet citizens whose small town is dominated by an ancient Cossack church. The cathedral becomes a symbol of the spiritual thirst of Ukrainians and their national memory, which no amount of Communist ideology can quench. The novel prompted a spirited response in Ukrainian *samvydav* (see page 75). During the era of *glasnost* Honchar became a staunch defender of language rights.

A radically new phenomenon, uncontrolled by the Party, was the appearance in the 1960s of a group of young writers labelled *shesty-desiatnyky*, the sixties. The group must be seen as a result of the struggle of 'children' against 'fathers,' a conflict that was not unknown in the socialist societies. The 'sons' could not forgive their 'fathers' for their humility towards Stalin, and they themselves felt unburdened by the grim realities of the past. The sixtiers were mostly poets, and included Vasyl Symonenko, Ivan Drach, Vitalii Korotych, Lina Kostenko, and Mykola Vinhranovsky. Stylistically they differed a great deal from one another, and did not form a single school. What united them was a new awareness of the function of poetry. They vigorously objected to the simplistic Soviet view of life and rediscovered human anguish and suffering as well as the fragility of human relationships. Their disenchantment rarely led them to a feeling of alienation. The forcefulness of their protests underscored their sense of engagement. Yet all paused to lift their voices to the level of 'eternal scores' (Drach) and to 'pass from soul to soul (from tongue to tongue) freedom of the spirit and the truth of the word' (Kostenko). Occasionally they succeeded. They did so in a language free from the clichés of the previous three decades, vibrant with new images and intricacies. Their achievement is all the more striking since it flew in the face of Khrushchev's pronouncements on literature in 1962, which tried to re-impose the straitjacket of *partiinost*.

A poet who, because of a distinct and more traditional style, stood a little apart from the sixtiers, was Vasyl Symonenko (1935–63). His first collection was *Tysha i hrim* (Silence and Thunder, 1962). *Zemne tiazhinnia* (Earth Gravity) appeared posthumously in 1964. A selection of his poems, some previously unpublished, and his diaries, *Bereh chekan* (The Edge of Anticipation), appeared in 1965 in New York. It may be regarded as the first appearance of Ukrainian *samvydav* (*samizdat*) abroad. It reveals Symonenko's great civic courage in openly denouncing in his poems the deep-seated vestiges of Stalinism. His uncompromising tone, his traditional style, and his deep love of Ukraine are reminiscent of Shevchenko. No wonder that long after his death he became a cult figure among young Ukrainians. In 1966 another collection of his verse appeared in Ukraine, but after that he was virtually banned. 'It is unjust,' wrote Mykola Zhulynsky in 1988, 'to keep silent not only about the works of this poet, who was a national conscience in Ukrainian literature, but also about his tragic fate. Symonenko was not destined to reach his full development, and the literary milieu in Cherkasy [the poet's home town] was not favourable to creative flights ...'[4]

The oldest of the sixtiers and the most talented was Lina Kostenko (b. 1930). Her first collection, *Prominnia zemli* (Earthly Rays), appeared in 1957. It was followed by *Vitryla* (Sails, 1958) and *Mandrivky sertsia* (The Wandering Heart, 1961). The collection *Zoriany intehral* (The Starry Integral), although it was announced for 1963, never appeared, and for a long time Kostenko remained silent. A master of the laconic and often aphoristic phrase, she is basically a lyric poet. It is the quiet, exploratory, inwardlooking direction of her best poems that so delighted the reader and infuriated the official critic. Only very occasionally do Kostenko's poems criticize Soviet society, where she finds 'many swindlers and sceptics,' especially among writers who love 'glory and comfort' ('Estafety'). Kostenko re-emerged during the era of *glasnost* (see page 84).

The most prominent of the sixtiers was Ivan Drach (b. 1936). In 1961 he published a long poem, *Nizh u sontsi* (Knife in the Sun), which created a sensation. It is a philosophical meditation on Ukrainian history, with the poet accompanied by the 'eternal devil.' His first collection of verse, *Soniashnyk* (Sunflower, 1962), confirmed his reputation as an intellectual poet of great originality. Drach's power lies in the daring use of association. In a preface to the collection Leonid Novychenko warned that this tendency might carry the poet beyond accepted Soviet norms and reflect his 'deep break with reality.'[5] It is true that Drach's thirst for discovering reality as it is, unvarnished by ideology, compels the reader to think independently. His other collections were *Protuberantsi sertsia* (Protuberances of the Heart, 1965) and *Do dzherel* (To the Sources, 1972). Drach has also translated into Ukrainian some poems by García Lorca, Norwid, Allen Ginsberg, and Voznesensky. He has continued to be published well into the era of *glasnost*.

Mykola Vinhranovsky (b. 1936) came to literature via film. His talent was first noted by Oleksander Dovzhenko. His first poems attracted attention by their strong evocation of nature in Ukraine. The collections of poems were many, among them *Atomni preliudy* (Atomic Preludes, 1962) and *Sto poezii* (A Hundred Poems, 1967). Vinhranovsky has also published collections of short stories.

Vitalii Korotych (b. 1936) is a doctor by profession. His first collection of poems, *Zoloti ruky* (Golden Hands), was published in 1961. Next came *Zapakh neba* (The Scented Sky, 1962), *Vulytsia voloshok* (The Street of Cornflowers, 1963), and *Techiia* (The Current, 1965). His poems ring with a deep sincerity, which by itself, of course, does not guarantee excellence. He is a committed writer, a member of the Communist Party, yet he is very sensitive to human problems. In 1965 he spent some time in Canada, describing the country in a reportage. His later career took him to Moscow as editor of *Ogonek*.

The young poets of the 1960s 'began a real revolution. Not only the patriotic and humanistic themes in their creative works were new, but the personal has been rehabilitated in poetry.'[6] An émigré critic published an anthology of sixty poets of the sixties[7] in which he listed many of those who joined this mass movement. Among them were Vasyl Holoborodko (b. 1942), Volodymyr Iavorivsky (b. 1942), Ihor Kalynets (b. 1939), Tamara Kolomiiets (b. 1935), Roman Kudlyk (b. 1941), Oles Lupii (b. 1938), Borys Mamaisur (b. 1938), Borys Necherda (b. 1939), Borys Oliinyk (b. 1935), Mykola Synhaivsky (b. 1936), Robert Tretiakov (b. 1936), Mykola Vorobiov (b. 1941), and Iryna Zhylenko (b. 1941). Most of them continued to publish their work during the Brezhnev era and many have survived until *glasnost*.

The most prominent prose writer among the sixtiers was Ievhen Hutsalo (b. 1937), one of the most talented short story writers of his generation. His collections were *Iabluka z osinnioho sadu* (Apples from an Autumn Orchard, 1964), *Skupana v liubystku* (Bathed in Lovage, 1965), and *Khustyna shovku zelenoho* (A Green Silk Kerchief, 1966). In one of his collections, *Peredchuttia radosti* (Intimations of Joy, 1972), he attempts to discuss some sensitive topics like religion and collaboration with the Germans during the war. Most of his stories deal with village life, but they deal with it in a manner that is not socialist-realist. His focus is on 'love of ordinary people, love of life in its not always visible complexity, a desire to discover the extraordinary in the ordinary, the festive in the everyday, the drama in comedy, and the life-affirming in tragedy. He shows great skill in creating an emotional atmosphere around a situation, the cobweb-like psychological picture of a good deed, the knowledge of an unseen logic in the movements of a character, the understanding and rewarding of an honest person, while unmasking the morally depraved.'[8]

In an interview Hutsalo said, 'the most significant period in my life was the second half of the 1960s, when I wrote the stories "Mertva zona" (The Dead Zone), "Rodynne vohnyshche" (The Family Hearth), "Silski vchyteli" (Village Teachers), "Podorozhni" (Travellers), which I regard as objective, realistic prose ... I am sorry that I did not move in this direction further. The reason was noisy criticism that wounded me.'[9]

The new wave of writers was greatly helped by the partial rehabilitation and republication of writers who perished in the purges. Among them were Antonenko-Davydovych, Bobynsky, Chechviansky, Dosvitnii, Drai-Khmara, Epik, Gzhytsky, Iohansen, Irchan, Khotkevych, Kosynka, Kulish, Kulyk, Kyrylenko, Mamontov, Mykytenko, Mysyk, Pluzhnyk, Polishchuk, Pylypenko, Shkurupii, Slisarenko, Vlyzko, Vyshnia, Zahul, and Zerov. Among those denied rehabilitation were Khvylovy, Pidmohylny, Semenko, and Svidzinsky. The rehabilitation process was conducted half-heartedly. Usually, one selected volume of the purged writer's works was published in a limited edition. The facts and details of the purges were never released, but covered up with euphemistic phrases like 'he left the ranks of Soviet literature.'

An important event in the late 1960s was the publication of an eight-volume history of Ukrainian literature. Volumes 6 and 7, which appeared in 1970 and 1971, covered Ukrainian literature up to the Second World War. The purges were not mentioned, but pages were devoted to those writers who later fell into disfavour – for example, seventeen pages to Khvylovy. This partial rehabilitation had lasting repercussions. The return of so many prominent names could not but stimulate the forces of renewal. Considering the severity of the repression in Ukraine, the regeneration of literature in the 1960s was truly remarkable. It spilled over into the prohibited channels of *samvydav*, which fuelled the dissident movement.

The dissident movement in Ukraine dates from 1964. In May of that year a fire destroyed part of the collection of the library of the Academy of Sciences in Kiev. A letter of protest was soon circulating in *samvydav*, blaming the KGB for instigating the fire. The document, like so many petitions, protests, and letters written in the next few years, demanded justice and freedom of speech, as well as criticizing the authorities for Russification and national discrimination. Some of the documents have literary and scholarly value. They stand on a par with works of poetry and fiction that also appeared in *samvydav*.

Foremost among the dissenters was the literary critic Ivan Dziuba (b. 1931), who in 1959 published a collection of essays, *Zvychaina liudyna chy mishchanyn*? (An Ordinary Man or a Philistine?). In 1964 he wrote an open letter to the secretary of the Communist Party of Ukraine, Petro Shelest, and enclosed his treatise *Internatsionalizm chy rusyfikatsiia*? (Internationalism or Russification?, published in English in London, 1968). Dziuba was primarily concerned with securing the civil liberties and cultural freedom promised by Lenin. His call was for a drastic reform of the Soviet system along Leninist principles, which, he argued, had been corrupted by Lenin's successors. Dziuba's masterful documentation of the Russification of Ukraine is the strength of the book. His first transgressions against the regime went unpunished because of his poor health and because Petro Shelest was half-inclined to listen to him. Later, however, these factors failed to keep him out of jail. Dziuba's career continued after his recantation and has lasted well into the period of *glasnost*.

The first wave of arrests of dissidents occurred in 1965, when among others the critic Ivan Svitlychny (b. 1929), the historian Valentyn Moroz (b. 1936), and the writer Mykhailo Osadchy (b. 1936) were placed under arrest. The secret trials of these men, held in 1966, the year of the Siniavsky-Daniel trial in Russia, attracted little attention abroad but produced an important collection of documents, similar to Ginzburg's 'white book,' by Viacheslav Chornovil (b. 1938) – *Lykho z rozumu* (Woe from Wit, Paris, 1967, translated as the *Chornovil Papers*, Toronto, 1968). The most interesting part of the collection deals with Soviet justice, or rather with the lack of justice, well documented by specific cases, interrogations, and eyewitness reports, collected by Chornovil.

A promising literary critic whose works found their way through clandestine channels was Ievhen Sverstiuk (b. 1928), author of *Sobor u ryshtuvanni* (Cathedral in Scaffolding, included in English in *Clandestine Essays*, Littleton, 1976). This is a long essay defending and interpreting Oles Honchar's novel *Sobor* (The Cathedral, 1968), which touched on vital problems of Ukrainian history. Sverstiuk pursues Honchar's historical observations to their logical conclusion and discusses in trenchant terms the Ukrainian national character, Ukrainian servility to foreign masters, and the absence of national pride in contemporary Ukraine. Yet his argument is not ultra-nationalist. He combines his concern for Ukraine with more universal themes of concern for ecology, education, and indeed, openness (*hlasnist*). However, for Sverstiuk, as for Solzhenitsyn in his Nobel Prize lecture, national literature has a moral and cognitive role to fulfil. Sverstiuk's essay on Ivan Kotliarevsky, 'Ivan Kotliarevsky smiietsia,' (Ivan Kotliarevsky Is Laughing) is a successful attempt to draw an analogy between the times of Kotliarevsky, when the very existence of Ukrainian literature was threatened by Russia, and the present day, when it is once more in danger of succumbing to Soviet Russian osmosis.

The historian Valentyn Moroz was an essayist with distinct literary qualities. His *Reportazh iz zapovidnyka Berii* (Report from the Beria Reservation, London, 1971) offers a superb analysis of totalitarianism, where everything is directed to produce a human cog (*hvyntyk*). Although at times reminiscent of Orwell, Moroz was an optimist, confident that his countrymen would allow themselves to be guided by *oderzhymist*, possessedness, or a national fanaticism. His other essays are *Khronika sprotyvu* (Chronicle of Resistance), *Moisei i Datan* (Moses and Datan), and *Sered snihiv* (Amid the Snows). Later Moroz was arrested, spent some time in a camp, but was released and allowed to go to the United States.

Two writers who were arrested and whose works circulated only in *samvydav* were Ihor Kalynets (b. 1939) and Mykhailo Osadchy (b. 1936). Kalynets was the author of *Vohon Kupala* (Kupalo's Fire), which was published in Kiev in 1966. Afterwards three collections appeared abroad: *Poezii z Ukrainy* (Poems from Ukraine, 1970), *Pidsumovuiuchy mov-*

channia (Summing-Up Silence, 1971), and *Koronuvannia opudala* (The Crowning of a Scarecrow, 1972). With great poetic virtuosity Kalynets evokes nostalgia for the past and reflects on religion, love, and the process of history. His last collection is a series of meditations without the slightest ideological overtone. Osadchy was the author of a striking autobiographical novel about concentration camp life, *Bilmo* (Cataract, New York, 1976). A very promising young poet who shared Kalynets's and Osadchy's fate was Hryhorii Chubai (1949–82), the author of a long Eliotesque poem 'Vidshukuvannia prychetnoho' (Search for an Accomplice). Chubai's best collection of poems, *Hovoryty, movchaty i hovoryty znovu* (To Speak, To Be Silent, and To Speak Again), was published posthumously in 1990.

After his release from the camp Borys Antonenko-Davydovych published a controversial novel about generational conflict, *Za shyrmoiu* (Behind the Screen, 1963), and a book of reminiscences, *Zdaleka i zblyzka* (From Far and Near, 1969).

In April 1972 Petro Shelest was removed from his position as first secretary of the Communist Party of Ukraine. This signalled the end of the 'thaw' and the tightening of controls on literature. In 1972 a second wave of arrests of dissidents swept across Ukraine. The victims were Sverstiuk, Stus, and many others, some arrested for the second time. The clandestine *Ukrainsky visnyk* (Ukrainian Herald), eight issues of which had appeared, was discontinued. In the words of Valerii Shevchuk, who came into prominence a little later,

Let us recall the political arrests of 1965 and 1972, let us recall that the post-sixtier poets were deliberately excluded from literature and that therefore literary development was crushed. Some of the sixtiers – M. Vinhranovsky, Iu. Shcherbak, I. Zhylenko, V. Symonenko, and the present author – were removed from the literary process; some found themselves behind bars – O. Berdnyk, V. Zakharchenko, A. Shevchuk, I. Svitlychny, V. Ruban, and others; the Ukrainian school of translators formed in the 1960s was destroyed; L. Kostenko remained silent, O. Honchar was ostracized because of his *Cathedral*, as well as B. Antonenko-Davydovych for his journalism. Ukrainian literature was thus not in a state of stagnation, like Russian, it was in a state of pogrom.[10]

Was it possible to return, under the stagnating regime of Leonid Brezhnev, to Stalinism? Fortunately, not.

5 From Stagnation to Reconstruction 1972–88

Both the ideological tendentiousness and the stultefying artistic sameness were seriously subverted by developments during the 'thaw.' The Soviet reader, fed on a diet of 'socialist realism' and saccharine Communist poetry came to savour a new and tastier menu. Contemporary literature, much of which remained unread, was suddenly supplemented by readable works. All this meant that despite the consolidation of power in the hands of Brezhnev and Suslov, the days of immaculate 'socialist realism' were numbered. Certainly, the old tendencies never quite disappeared, and among the faithful 'socialist realists' who churned out the familiar stuff were many writers – among them Vasyl Bolshak, Mykola Ishchenko, Rostyslav Sambuk, and Iurii Zbanatsky and a host of others – who need not detain us. The poems about Lenin, the novels about the civil war and collectivization, as well as about Second World War heroism, continued to be written with the old Communist zeal. The perennial defamation of Ukrainian nationalists was still an important priority. 'To fight against these traitors,' wrote Pavlo Zahrebelny in 1981, 'to unmask them before the entire world is one of the most noble tasks of our literature.'[1] One must never come to terms with the defeated enemy.

A good example of 'socialist realism' with a new face is provided by the work of Vasyl Zemliak (1923–77), author of the award-winning novels *Lebedyna zhraia* (The Swan Flock, 1971) and *Zeleni Mlyny* (1976). According to the official blurb with which all Soviet works are now provided, the novels 'portray a wide canvas that embraces the period from the first organization of communes to the victorious fulfilment of the great patriotic war.' This 'restructuring of the Ukrainian village' is described without any mention of the great famine, but in a manner 'steeped with humour, some good irony, smiles, a broad application of relative scepticism, the use of mythology and allegory, and in general searching out more effective imagery and innovative form.'[2] It was not until 1988 that the deep cuts the novels were subjected to at the time of publication were revealed in the press. The editors of these editions admitted that 'they were forced to leave out of the work many of the author's thoughts, some episodes, and even whole chapters that were unacceptable at that time ... In the chapter 'Holodni koni' (Hungry Horses) Vasyl Zemliak tells of the famine of 1933, an event so tragic and so cruel that it cannot be omitted from the epic story of that time.'[3] Perhaps a revised edition with all the omissions restored would enhance this work, which in its general thrust remains 'socialist realist.'

A much more talented prose writer was Hryhir Tiutiunnyk (1931–80), author of many collections of short stories. Among them are *Zaviaz* (Buds, 1966), *Derevii* (Yarrow, 1969), *Batkivski porohy* (The Parents' Threshold, 1972), and *Kholodna miata* (Cool Mint, in English, 1986). Like Chekhov's depiction of the barbarism of Russian village life, Tiutiunnyk's art focuses on the dark side of a Ukrainian village after the Second World War. 'Soft-spoken, and the possessor of a refined lyrical vision, Hryhir Tiutiunnyk could often be scathing and ruthless. His stories breathe a withering sarcasm and scorn when he dwells on characters who disregard the moral standards of socialist society, defile their consciences and the wisdom of national traditions, and aspire to live the totally egotistical lives of grabbers and parasites.'[4] Tiutiunnyk's life, we read in an article published during the Gorbachev thaw, 'was devilishly hard, his writing difficult, followed by inevitable harsh strictures in print ... The nameless heroes of criticism looked at his texts with a magnifying glass, searching for ideological deviations and, upon them, thoroughly castrated him.'[5] Harassed and hounded, Tiutiunnyk took his own life on 5 March 1980.

Iurii Shcherbak (b. 1934) is a physician who started writing prose in the 1960s. Among his works are *Iak na viini* (As in Wartime, 1966) and *Malenka futbolna komanda* (A Small Football Team, 1973). He is also the author of a major novel, *Barier nesumisnosti* (The Barrier of Incompatibility, 1971), in which he wanted to 'show the role of contingency, illogicality, and unpredictability in human actions.'[6] Shcherbak's work has strong existentialist overtones. He also represents the strengthening of the philosophical and ethical trend in artistic depictions of the world ... The human being had to be alienated for a time from reality in order to break the customary ways of looking at the world, to destroy the stereotypes and clichés. The use of the hyperbolic and grotesque, the introduction of fantastic images, folk-tales, and legends was implemented by a desire to stop for a while the uninterrupted process of life and to lead a character beyond his limits in order to evoke different reflections and thus stimulate the need for a philosophical reassessment of man and the world.'[7]

Shcherbak took an active part in the ecological debates of the 1980s and wrote about the catastrophe at Chernobyl.

Valerii Shevchuk (b. 1939) is another writer whose career suffered under Brezhnev's 'stagnation.' He is the author of *Naberezhna 12* (12, The Esplanade, 1968), full of existential overtones, and *Vechir sviatoi oseni* (A Blessed Autumn Evening, 1969). During the 1970s Shevchuk concentrated on translating Ukrainian medieval and baroque texts into modern Ukrainian. In 1979 he published a collection of short stories, *Kryk pivnia na svitanku* (Cockcrow at Dawn), and a novel, *Na poli smyrennomu* (On a Submissive Field), in which he ventured into the supernatural. A great mythological prose achievement was *Dim na hori* (The House on the Hill, 1983). Then in 1986 he was awarded a prize for his fine historical novel, *Try lystky za viknom* (Three Leaves outside the Window). Writing of Shevchuk's mythological, religious, and philosophical topoi, Marko Pavlyshyn argues:

Shevchuk has created readings of the past that are not guided by the beacon of state ideology, that do not reiterate the thesis of the beneficent centrality of Moscow, and that allude to a former wealth, autonomy, and dignity of Ukrainian culture ... Shevchuk is far more radical. He seeks an alternative to authority itself: escape from the world's structures; the baroque ideal most frequently invoked in the first two narratives of *Try lystky*, might well serve as an emblem of his work as a whole. It is, therefore, with the purpose of transcending immutable and exclusive hierarchies of cultural values that Shevchuk's prose delivers to the reader materials that might help shape a new Ukrainian cultural identity or identities.[8]

'The novel *Na poli smyrennomu*,' declared Shevchuk in an interview, 'is to be the first in a cycle of historical tales (or novels, I am not sure of the definition) in which I want to trace the history of the human psyche (not in general, but the one that is dear to me) throughout the course of the history of my people ... Perhaps it will take my entire life to write this book.'[9]

Another writer who could have said the same thing is Roman Ivanychuk (b. 1929). His first historical novel, *Malvy* (Hollyhocks, 1969), dealing with the problem of 'janissarism' (a loss of national memory), was severely criticized and subsequently banned. In an interview he declared, 'the past is an inseparable part of our being; we always stand between the past and the future, as if in the centre of a circle, and if the most terrible thing should happen – the loss of human memory – mankind would be unable to respond to the world, to pass on the experience it has gained, which is coded in love and hate, to the next generation, and therefore mankind would lose its future.'[10]

Ivanychuk's other historical novels were *Cherlene vyno* (Red Wine, 1977), about the siege of a castle in the fifteenth century; *Manuskrypt z vulytsi ruskoi* (Manuscript from Ruska Street, 1979), about Lviv in the sixteenth century; *Voda z kameniu* (Water from a Stone, 1981), about Markian Shashkevych; *Chetverty vymir* (The Fourth Dimension, 1984), about the Cyrillo-Methodian Mykola Hulak; *Shramy na skali* (Scratches on Rock, 1987), about Ivan Franko; and *Zhuravlyny kryk* (The Call of the Cranes, 1988), about the Zaporozhian *otaman*, Kalnyshevsky. The latter book appeared more than a decade after it was written. The novels of Ivanychuk do not illustrate, but rather relive, history and have found a warm response among many readers.

A novelist of much wider range, but whose greater achievement is also in the historical genre, is Pavlo Zahrebelny (b. 1924). Having started with propagandist novels against the West – *Evropa – 45* (Europe – 45, 1959), *Evropa – Zakhid* (Europe – West, 1961) – and against the nationalists – *Shepit* (1966) – he moved on to history in his novel *Dyvo* (Marvel, 1968). The composition of *Dyvo*, which focuses on the construction of St Sophia Cathedral in Kiev, 'resembles the architecture of the cathedral, which is imaginatively depicted in the novel. The unusual plans, transitions, additions, devil-may-care assymetry, are hidden in purposefulness and harmony. Everything resembles a native song.'[11] The overall tendency of the novel is 'to show the indestructibility of national history, through which all that is good enters our spiritual heritage and favours the formation of the Communist mentality of the Soviet man.'[12]

Zahrebelny's narration touches on what, in Milan Kundera's terms, a novel ought to do: 'A novel examines not reality but existence.'[13] The same is true of the three following novels: *Ievpraksiia* (1974), *Roksoliana* (1979), and *Ia, Bohdan* (I, Bohdan, 1982). 'Ievpraksiia and Roksoliana led a fight to save their personalities, their dignity, their fate, and they excelled spiritually because they were victorious. This only happened because their struggle was nurtured by love for their native land, and the hope of seeing it helped them to preserve their personalities, prevented them from being absorbed by a foreign environment.'[14]

The novel about Bohdan Khmelnytsky created a great stir. 'We have not seen any work like this in Ukraine. Disputes, confessions, polemics, philosophical generalizations, and human reflections – all this against a background of epochal historical events, in fact, in the thick of these events, which are portrayed not in objective sequence but transformed by the hero's consciousness, interpreted in the light of painful questions, asked both of himself and the reader, considered from the point of view of the hero's own times and from the pinnacle of our age.'[15] Although Khmelnytsky is still praised for the union with Russia at Pereiaslav, he is also hailed as the creator of the Ukrainian nation. While acknowledging this, Marko Pavlyshyn persuasively states his caveat against the novel:

How should one evaluate the novel? The easiest way out would be to use the most popular silent understanding of literary criticism: it is good that the work is complex, erudite, and during its analysis suggests to the critic many thoughts. According to these criteria *Ia, Bohdan* is undoubtedly an important and valuable work. But for the reader who is used to the cultural and literary traditions of the West the work will appear too dull and too slow. Its style and structure are masterfully mannered, but the entire tone is solemnly serious, without the slightest playfulness, irony, or self-parody. The content offers nothing unexpected or novel. There are too few open problems that could lead to a wide discussion. All the basic questions have found authoritative answers in extraliterary dimension, and the novel only explains them. True, this apologist ritual is performed with great skill. But this is a feature of medieval hagiography, not of a modern novel.[16]

In 1988 Zahrebelny published a mildly controversial novel, *Pivdenny komfort* (Southern Comfort).

A writer whose great potential was only half-realized is Volodymyr Drozd (b. 1939). He is the author of two collections of short stories, *Maslyny* (Olives, 1967) and *Bily kin Sheptalo* (The White Horse Sheptalo, 1969), and two novels, *Yrii* (Fantasy Land, 1974) and *Spektakl* (A Spectacle, 1985).

In the novels, novellas, and short stories of Volodymyr Drozd conscience is a kind of barometer that measures the pressure of the moral atmosphere of society, in a micro situation, in one's own awareness of the world, in one's thoughts, emotions, and actions. Conscience may be civic-minded and brave but it may also be helpless, it may capitulate before an irrepressible thirst for glory, well-being, blind careerism. Drozd meditates on the problems of bravery and the helplessness of conscience in his novellas *Balada pro Slastiona* and *Samotnii vovk* ... Volodymyr Drozd unmasked in an artistically original and civically uncompromising way widespread antisocial and amoral phenomena – opportunism, careerism, demagogic speculation in contemporary issues, and social parasitism. Using a form of monologue he 'forced' the reality in the person of the narrator to condemn the appearance of 'Slastionovism,' to recreate the process of its upward rise and moral collapse. *Samotnii vovk* is permeated with the pathos of the dismemberment of the egocentric mentality and behaviour of ... Andrii Shyshyha, who, through hypocrisy and opportunism, tries to reach the pinnacle of social well-being.[17]

In the novel *Spektakl* Drozd tries to analyse the career of a Soviet writer. 'There are many features in the spiritual and moral conformism of the writer Iaroslav Petrunia. Petrunia himself would not look back at his past if he could, without doubts, categorically say to himself: "It was there and then that I chose the path of compromise with conscience for ephemeral fame, comfort, official prestige, and so lost my real self.'[18] It would be unjust to regard this and other works of Drozd simply as a mirror of contemporary Soviet society with its positive and negative aspects. His strength lies in the polyphonic, whimsical, and grotesque form that makes his novels truly modern. Perhaps, in the atmosphere of *glasnost*, he will write a truly great novel – this is within his reach.

Iurii Mushketyk (b. 1929) is the author of several popular novels written in a traditional, non-experimental style. Among them are the historical novels *Semen Palii* (1954) and *Iasa* (Radiance, 1987), about the Zaporozhian *koshovy*, Ivan Sirko. Sometimes his works are written in direct response to Party policy – for example, *Sertse i kamin* (Heart and Stone), outlining the new agricultural policy – or to a problem that the Party presents for discussion – as in *Den prolitaie nad namy* (Day Passes over Us, 1967), about Soviet youth. *Zhorstoke myloserdia* (Cruel Mercy, 1973) is about German fascism.

'The ability to gain self-knowledge and a correct evaluation of oneself is, according to the author, not some relative objective, but a guarantee of eternal constructive effort, the object of which is man himself. To create oneself does not mean to change one's soul basically, to orient one's inner "I" to something quite different, it means to achieve one's own personal level, to learn to live a moral life.'[19] Mushketyk's concept of morality is, of course, Soviet, permeated with the ideals of collectivism and optimism. This he reveals in his 'village prose' piece, *Pozytsiia* (Position, 1982), which was awarded a prize. The novel *Vernysia v dim svii* (Return to Your Home, 1981) and many of his short stories are dedicated to this 'moral search.' Mushketyk is a sophisticated 'socialist realist,' forever sensitive to the latest twist and turn of the Party line.

There are several prose writers of the second rank who have become prominent in the past two decades. Among them is Oles Lupii (b. 1938), who made his literary debut as a poet. In his novels and short stories, full of cardboard characters – *Hran* (The Edge, 1968), *Vidlunnia osinnioho hromu* (The Echo of Autumn Thunder, 1976), *Nikomu tebe ne viddam* (I Won't Give you Back to Anyone, 1984) – he depicts life in his native Western Ukraine. Lupii has also written film scenarios.

Nina Bichuia (b. 1937) is a talented prose writer also from Western Ukraine. Bichuia has written stories for children as well as a collection of prose, *Rodovid* (Lineage, 1984), and a 'novel-essay' about Kulish and Kurbas, *Desiat sliv poeta* (Ten Words of a Poet, 1987).

Yet another well-known writer from Western Ukraine is Roman Fedoriv (b. 1930), the long-time editor of the Lviv journal *Zhovten* (October, now renamed *Dzvin*, The Bell). He is the author of several collections of short stories and the novels *Zhban vyna* (A Pitcher of Wine, 1968), *Kamiane pole* (Stony Field, 1978), and *Zhorna* (Millstones, 1983). Especially evocative of the Galician past is the 'novel-essay' *Tanets chuhaistra* (Chuhaister's Dance, 1984). Despite occasional journalistic sallies against Ukrainian émigrés, Fedoriv, in the words of a critic, 'represents a movement into history, historical memory, and the historic roots of the people.'[20] Stepan Pushyk (b. 1944) is a promising prose writer from Western Ukraine who wrote the short novel *Pero zolotoho ptakha* (The Feather of a Golden Bird, 1978) and the historical 'novel-essay' *Halytska brama* (Galician Gate, 1988).

A Transcarpathian writer of some reputation is Ivan Chendei (b. 1922), author of many short stories and the novels *Ptakhy polyshaiut hnizda* (Birds Are Leaving Their Nests, 1965) and *Krynychna voda* (Well Water, 1980). The former novel attempts to show 'how socialism came to a Transcarpathian village.' Chendei 'revealed a need to preserve a harmonious balance between the past and the present, the present and the future in natural, spiritual terms.'[21]

An original prose writer of great versatility is Volodymyr Iavorivsky. As well as some short stories and journalism he wrote the novels *Ohliansia z oseni* (Turn Back from Autumn, 1979), *A teper idy* (Now, Go, 1983), *Avtoportret z uiavy* (An Imaginary Self-Portrait, 1984), and *Druhe pryshestiia* (The Second Coming, 1986). His art is 'generous in laughter, jokes, humour, parody, burlesque, grotesque, and fantasy.'[22]

Serhii Plachynda (b. 1928) is the author of *Kyivski fresky* (Kievan Frescoes, 1982) and a novelistic biography of Iurii Ianovsky (1986). He is at present an activist in the Ukrainian ecological movement and a fighter for linguistic rights.

The poets of the era of stagnation did less well than the prose writers. The reasons were openly described in 1988: 'Gross administrative intervention in the literary process, artificial limitations placed on freedom of creation, and ruthless interference by a whole army of officials in purely literary affairs during the period of stagnation forced the poets to be very cautious, to watch out for the man with the briefcase, and to come to terms with conformism in their environment.'[23]

A prominent poet, who started her career in the 1960s, was Lina Kostenko, who had great difficulty in publishing her poems. Her historical novel in verse, *Marusia Churai*, appeared in 1979, but it was not acclaimed and awarded the Shevchenko prize until 1987. In 1980 she published a collection of poems, *Nepovtornist* (Not to Be Repeated), and in 1987, *Sad netanuchykh skulptur* (The Orchard of Indestructible Sculpture). Some of her poems (*Berestechko*), written in 1970, were published for the first time in the era of *glasnost*. Today, Kostenko is the undisputed reigning poet of Ukraine.

Platon Voronko (1913–88) was a Communist true believer who received many prizes for his collections of poems. Among them were *U svitli blyskavyts* (In the Light of Lightning, 1968), *Zdvyh-zemlia* (Victorious Earth, 1976), and *Sovist pamiati* (The Conscience of Memory, 1980). In his imitations of folk poetry he remained an eternal optimist. Stepan Oliinyk (1908–82) was known for his satiric verses directed against idle peasants and foreign imperialists. Some of his barbs hit out at Soviet philistinism in defence of 'Communist morality.' A poet born in Western Ukraine, who sometimes attempted to go beyond 'socialist realism,' was Dmytro Pavlychko (b. 1929). His early nonconformism was seen in his collection *Pravda klyche* (Truth Is Calling, 1957), which was banned. Subsequent collections in the 1960s and 1970s included some good sonnets in *Bili sonety* (The White Sonnets), *Kyivski sonety* (Kievan Sonnets), and *Sonety podilskoi oseni* (Sonnets of the Podillian Autumn). He is concerned with 'eternal problems: good and evil, love and hate, life and death, labour, creativity, and human happiness.'[24] Pavlychko is also known as a translator. In the era of *glasnost* he has become one of the leaders of Rukh and has left the Communist Party. A more orthodox poet is Borys Oliinyk (b. 1935), author of the collections *Vybir* (Choice, 1965), *Vidlunnia* (Echo, 1970), and many others. He has also written poems about Lenin. In *Zaklynannia vohniu* (Incantation of Fire, 1978) he lashed out against the United States.

Two dramatists, celebrated in the earlier decades but not innovative, should be mentioned: Mykola Zarudny (b. 1921) and Oleksii Kolomiets (b. 1919). Kolomiets' *Planeta Speranta* (The Planet of Hope, 1965) attracted much publicity. Oleksander Levada's *Faust i smert* (Faust and Death, 1960) was another popular play in the sixties and seventies.

A poet of the first rank, who was incarcerated in the 1970s and died in a concentration camp in Perm oblast, was Vasyl Stus (1938–85). As a martyr he has become a cult figure in Ukraine. Collections of his poems were published in the West: *Zymovi dereva* (Trees in Winter, 1970), *Svicha v svichadi* (A Candle in a Mirror, 1977), and *Palimpsesty* (Palimpsests, 1986). After 1989 many of his poems were published in Ukraine, and a complete collection of his poetry is in preparation. Born of anguish and suffering in the camps, his poetry is directed at his homeland. In the words of George Shevelov, it is 'unprogrammatic poetry ... which can endlessly vary around the same theme and normally remains lyrical. Its richness lies in the variety of experience and in its intensity.'[25] Another critic pointed out that Stus's 'prison poetry is permeated with Shevchenko's thoughts, his power, courage, and rebelliousness.'[26] The impact of Stus's poetry on the contemporary Ukrainian reader is very significant.

Several poets of the same generation – Vasyl Holoborodko, Borys Necherda, Vasyl Ruban, Iryna Zhylenko, and others – had their best poems banned, censored, and mutilated. Another victim of the 1970s repression was the poet Mykola Rudenko (b. 1920). He was arrested in 1977 for founding the Ukrainian Helsinki Group. After serving a sentence in a camp he was allowed to emigrate to the United States, where most of his collections of poems were published; some titles are *Prozrinnia* (Sight Returned, 1978) and *Za gratamy* (Behind Bars, 1980). According to a critic, Rudenko's poetry, pedestrian at first, showed some 'richness in cosmological and philosophical themes.'[27] He was also the author of a novel, *Orlova balka* (Eagle's Valley, 1982).

Oles Berdnyk (b. 1927) began as a science fiction writer and ended as a *sui generis* Christian fundamentalist. He spent many years in a concentration camp. Outstanding among his many works are *Okotsvit* (Eye-Flower, 1970) and *Zoriany korsar* (Stellar Corsair, 1971). Some of his *samvydav* works – for example, *Sviata Ukraina* (Sacred Ukraine, 1980) – have been published in the West.

An original poet who avoided a brush with Soviet law was Pavlo Movchan (b. 1939), the author of the collections *Kora* (Bark, 1968), *Holos* (Voice, 1982), *Zholud* (Acorn, 1983), *Porih* (Threshold, 1988), and *Sil* (Salt, 1989). 'The basic concepts of his poetic text,' writes Ivan Dziuba, 'are movement, space and time – the prime elements of being. Concentration on these elements is a mark of a philosophical poet.'[28] In the era of *glasnost* Movchan has become politically active.

By 1985 literature in Ukraine showed signs of exhaustion. The approaching political crisis was to some extent foreshadowed by the decay of literary works. New ideas were needed to revive the literary process. A national renewal was just around the corner.

6 Western Ukraine and Emigration 1919–39

After the First World War some Ukrainian provinces remained outside Soviet Ukraine, under Polish, Czechoslovak, and Romanian rule. Galicia, Volhynia, and Polisiia came to be part of Poland; Transcarpathia, part of Czechoslovakia; and Bukovina, part of Romania. In all these lands the development of Ukrainian language, education, and literature was hindered by various government measures. Yet, relatively speaking, these areas enjoyed greater creative freedom and an absence of direct political controls. The most advanced in many respects was Galicia with its capital city of Lviv. Here, early in the 1920s, several literary groups sprang up.

A special place in Galician literature is occupied by those poets who were in the ranks of the Ukrainski Sichovi Striltsi, the Ukrainian Sharpshooters. Lev Lepky, Roman Kupchynsky, and others wrote poems that were often turned into songs. They were published in the journal *Shliakhy* (Pathways, 1915). Roman Kupchynsky ((1894–1976) was also the author of a prose trilogy, *Zametil* (Snowstorm, 1928–30), and humorous feuilletons that he published in *Dilo* (Deed) under the penname Halaktion Chipka. The long dramatic poem *Velyky den* (A Great Day, 1921) was less successful.

The modernist group Mytusa was formed around the journal of that name published in 1922 and edited by Vasyl Bobynsky, who later emigrated to Soviet Ukraine. Apart from Bobynsky, Shkrumeliak, Holubets, and Pidhirianka, a prominent poet of the group was Oles Babii (1897–1975), author of several collections of poems: *Nenavyst i liubov* (Hate and Love, 1921), *Hniv* (Anger, 1922), *Hutsulsky kurin* (The Hutsul Detachment, 1928), and erotic verses, *Za shchastia omanoiu* (Happiness through Delusion, 1930). He gradually abandoned modernist verse in favour of patriotic poetry and prose. A remarkable anti-war novel, *Poza mezhamy boliu* (Beyond the Limits of Pain, 1922), was written by Osyp Turiansky (1880–1933).

Among the Galician writers in the 1920s were many Sovietophiles. They centred around the journals *Novi shliakhy* (New Pathways, 1929–32), *Krytyka* (1933), and *Vikna* (Windows, 1928–32). One of the foremost among them was Antin Krushelnytsky, whose major works appeared before the First World War and who came to the pro-Soviet camp via the nationalist route; he was a cabinet minister in the Ukrainian People's Republic. In 1934 he emigrated to Soviet Ukraine, only to be arrested a year later. Iaroslav Halan (1902–49), who also belonged to the Sovietophile group Horno, was a journalist and pamphleteer rather than a serious writer. Among his plays are *Don Kikhot z Etenhaima* (Don Quixote from Ettenheim, 1927) and *99%* (1930). He was assassinated by a Ukrainian nationalist. Stepan Tudor (1892–1941) was the author of the novels *Maria* (1930) and *Den otsia Soiky* (The Day of Father Soika, 1932–47), an anti-Vatican tirade. Oleksander Havryliuk (1911–41) wrote a short story, 'Naivny muryn' (The Naive Black Man, 1930), and Petro Kozlaniuk (1904–65) was the author of the collection of short stories *Khlopski harazdy* (The Peasant Woes, 1927) and the trilogy *Iurko Kruk* (1934–56). On the whole, this group of writers left behind little of merit, except in journalism and satire.

To counter the Sovietophiles two nationalist groups of writers appeared, with a much larger following. The first of them was an organization of Catholic writers, Lohos (Logos). Their leader was the critic Hryhor Luzhnytsky. From 1930 to 1939 works by the members of Lohos were published in the journal *Dzvony* (Bells), edited by Mykola Hnatyshak and Petro Isaiv.

This journal also published the works of the talented prose writer, Natalena Koroleva (1888–1966), who lived in Czechoslovakia. She wrote the historical prose works *Vo dni ony* (Once upon a Time, 1935, *1313* (1935) and *Legendy starokyivski* (Ancient Kievan Legends, 1942–3).

Works of the best poet of the entire generation, Bohdan Ihor Antonych (1909–37), a native of the Lemko region, were also published in *Dzvony*. Antonych's collections of poems were *Pryvitannia zhyttia* (Greetings to Life, 1931), *Try persteni* (Three Rings, 1934), *Knyha Leva* (The Book of the Lion, 1936), *Zelena ievanheliia* (The Green Evangelium,

1938), and *Rotatsii* (Rotations, 1938). The imagist poetry of Antonych is summed up by Bohdan Rubchak:

From his second book onward, Antonych was carefully orchestrating every collection by excluding much more material than he included. His selections were not motivated by quality alone, since some of the poems that were left out are obviously better than many of those which made it into the books. They were motivated by the *persona* that Antonych was carefully constructing – the *persona* of the poet as Orpheus. The haunting poem 'The Home beyond a Star' is its crowning chord. This poem proclaims the unity of earth and horizon, of immediacy and distance, of transcendence and immanence. But above all it proclaims the unity of poetry and the world.[1]

The great beauty of Antonych's poems was instantly recognized by both critics and readers. After 1939, however, he was declared to be a 'bourgeois nationalist' and his works were banned in Soviet Ukraine until 1967, when a collected edition was published in Kiev. In the same year the collected works of Antonych appeared in New York, and in 1966 in Bratislava. Now his reputation in Ukraine seems to be secure.

A group of poets with a decidedly nationalist orientation gathered around the journal *Visnyk* (The Herald, 1933–9), edited by a distinguished critic, the father of Ukrainian 'integral nationalism,' Dmytro Dontsov (1883–1973). The leading poet of this group, Ievhen Malaniuk (1897–1968) was born in Kherson province in Ukraine and served as an officer in the army of the Ukrainian People's Republic. He emigrated in 1920, and in the period between the wars lived mostly in Prague and Warsaw. His collections of poetry include *Stylet i stylos* (Stiletto and Stilo, 1925), *Herbarii* (Herbarium, 1926), *Zemlia i zalizo* (Earth and Steel, 1930), *Zemna Madonna* (The Earthly Madonna, 1934), and *Persten Polikrata* (The Ring of Polycrates, 1939).

Even in his first collection, *Stylet i stylos*, Malaniuk threw down the gauntlet to everything coming from Russia and to everything weak and feeble in the Ukrainian psyche. He contrasted the strength, manliness, and will of the Ukrainians with their weaknesses, their love of singing, their mawkishness and love of peace, comparing these characteristics to Rome on the one hand to Greece on the other. The poet must [according to him] form his nation, building in the hearts of his readers a firm and uncompromising national consciousness ... Yet a poet of Malaniuk's stature would not do so by being merely a fighter, a builder, or an ideologue. He must also talk of the universal, that is, of the personal. Malaniuk is conscious of this Janus-like bifurcation and sometimes mentions it in his works. At a time when the poet as a tribune must be strong, proud, and dedicated to his ideal – the poet as a human being is conscious of his solitude, his helplessness in the face of the universe.[2]

Malaniuk continued writing during the second emigration to the United States (see page 98).

A writer who regularly contributed to *Visnyk* but who lived in Germany was the old neoclassicist Iurii Klen (pseudonym of Osvald Burkhardt, 1891–1947). In 1937 he published in Lviv a long poem, *Prokliati roky* (The Cursed Years). He continued to write after the Second World War.

Bohdan Kravtsiv (1904–75), who belonged to a secret organization of Ukrainian nationalists, lived in Lviv and was a member of the *Visnyk* group. His collections of poems were *Doroha* (The Way, 1929), *Promeni* (Sun Rays, 1930), and *Sonety i strofy* (Sonnets and Stanzas, 1933). 'Kravtsiv's first two collections are neoromantic. Artistically he comes close to the poetry of Vlyzko, Ianovsky, and the early Rylsky. These works are full of optimism, a desire to travel, a longing for distant exotic lands. One can see here the "vitaism" of Soviet poetry of the 1920s and 1930s on the one hand, and the optimism, voluntarism, and some formal features of the Visnykists, like Malaniuk, on the other.'[3] In his third collection Kravtsiv emerged as an accomplished neoclassicist. After the war he continued his career in the United States.

A scholarly young archaelogist who became a distinguished poet, ideologically close to *Visnyk*, was Oleh Olzhych (1908–44). Son of the modernist poet Oles, he lived in Prague and later became one of the leaders of the Ukrainian nationalist underground. His collections of verse are *Rin* (Gravel, 1935), *Vezhi* (Towers, 1940), and *Pidzamcha* (1946). In his poetry 'purely romantic themes, permeated by heavy symbolism, are curbed by the frame of the classical form. His best poems tell of mankind's past, of the prehistory and early history of Western civilization.'[4] In 1944 Olzhych was tortured to death by the Nazis.

Olzhych's tragic fate was shared by another talented poet, Olena Teliha (1907–42), who lived in Prague and Warsaw and contributed to *Visnyk*. She was shot by the Germans. A collection of her verse, *Dusha na storozhi* (A Soul on Guard), was published posthumously in 1946. Teliha, whose poetry is a strange mixture of nationalist fervour and feminine emotion, has become a cult figure.

A poet of great stature, who lived in Prague but was published by *Visnyk*, was Oleksa Stefanovych (1899–1970). His collections are *Poezii* (Poems, 1927) and *Stephanos I* (1938). 'All Stefanovych's works demonstrate the great range of his talent, the wide horizons of his scanty *oeuvre*, underlined by sharp contrasts. The flowering and ripening of nature is opposed to a world-destroying desert. There is the richness, full-bloodedness, and eroticism of life, as well as the bony, Holbein-like dances of death. There are hymns to a woman's body and clear mystical visions.'5

Among those poets who emigrated to Central Europe there was, for a while, a 'Prague school.' A prominent member of this group, besides Teliha and others, was Iurii Darahan (1894–1926), the author of a single collection, *Sahaidak* (A Quiver, 1925). A leading star, who was also a talented sculptor, was Oksana Liaturynska (1902–70). Her collections of poetry were *Husla* (Psaltery, 1938) and *Kniazha emal* (Princely Enamel, 1941). A superb craftsman, Liaturynska had a vision 'of an ancient separateness of Ukrainian spirituality, which showed itself best in folk art and which she believed must be preserved at all costs. Liaturynska saw this spirituality as "pantheism, an ideal world view, the search for eternal values, rooted in one's own soul, which create a new world ..."6

A Prague poet who followed a 'lyric-Epicurean' philosophy was Mykola Chyrsky (1903–42), the author of the collection *Emal* (Enamel, 1941). Lavro Myroniuk (1887–?) was a very talented émigré poet who met a tragic fate. He spent most of his time in mental hospitals in Prague and Vienna. He did not publish a collection of verse, and most of his poems that have survived were saved by friends. Many of his themes are religious, and his metaphors are very forceful and sometimes surrealist. Some critics compare him to Kafka.

Another centre of émigré writers was Warsaw. Here Iurii Lypa (1900–44) formed the group called Tank. A doctor and an amateur scholar, Lypa left three collections of poetry: *Svitlist* (Radiance, 1925), *Suvorist* (Sternness, 1931), and *Viruiu* (Credo, 1938). He is an original poet, but his main achievement lies in his prose: the novel *Kozaky v Moskovii* (Cossacks in Muscovy, 1934), short stories in *Notatnyk* (Sketch-

book, 1936–7), and essays *Bii za ukrainsku literaturu* (The Battle of
Ukrainian Literature, 1935) and *Pryznachennia Ukrainy* (Ukraine's Destiny, 1938). In his prose works Lypa preached integral nationalism with
racial overtones. He was tortured to death by the Communists.

The leading poet of the Warsaw group was Natalia Livytska-Kholodna (b. 1902), the author of masterly erotic poems in *Vohon i popil*
(Fire and Ashes, 1934) and patriotic verse in *Sim liter* (Seven Letters,
1937). In the 1930s she belonged to a group called My (We) in Warsaw,
which centred around the magazine of that name. Livytska-Kholodna
reached the apogee of her fame as a poet in her old age in the United
States (see page 99).

A literary magazine published in the 1930s in Lviv, *Nazustrich* (Encounter), provided a platform for some Galician writers. The leading
theoretician of the group was the brilliant literary critic Mykhailo Rudnytsky (1889–1975), the author of collections of poems, *Ochi ta usta*
(Eyes and Mouth, 1932); of short stories, *Nahody i pryhody* (Occasions
and Adventures, 1929); and of essays, *Vid Myrnoho do Khvylovoho* (Between Myrny and Khvylovy, 1936). The best poet in the group was
Sviatoslav Hordynsky (b. 1906). Hordynsky was the prolific author of
the collections *Barvy i linii* (Colours and Lines, 1933), *Buruny* (Storms,
1936), *Slova na kameniakh* (Words on Stones, 1937), *Viter nad poliamy*
(Wind over the Fields, 1938), *Lehendy hir* (Legends about Mountains,
1939), and *Sim lit* (Seven Years, 1939). 'In Hordynsky's poetry one can
see, on the one hand, great erudition and, on the other, wide interests.
In other words he is an eclectic poet. We find in his rich poetry several
types crossing and separating, but never merging. It is, therefore, difficult to talk about his creations as a complete monolithic poetic world.'[7]
Hordynsky, an accomplished painter, is also known as a translator and
an amateur scholar.

Iurii Kosach (1909–90) was an original talent in prose, poetry, and
drama. He lived in Warsaw and Paris. His collections of poems were
Cherlen (Redness, 1935) and *Myt z maistrom* (A Moment with the Master,
1936). There were also collections of novellas – *Sontse skhodyt v Chy-
hyryni* (The Sun Rises in Chyhyryn, 1934) and *Dyvymos v ochi smerti*
(We Look Death in the Eyes, 1936) – and of short stories – *Charivna
Ukraina* (Enchanting Ukraine, 1937) and *Klubok Ariadny* (Ariadne's Knot,
1937). 'Iurii Kosach is a versatile writer. His works, in many genres, are
permeated with his restless personality and a colourful, though some-

times journalistic, style. Yet often he leaves his work unfinished and displays too many literary influences. As a result, his achievement, although sometimes brilliant, is rather uneven.'[8]

The most promising novelist in Galicia in the 1930s was Ulas Samchuk (1905–88), the author of a trilogy, *Volyn* (Volhynia, 1932–7). The work 'portrayed the collective image of a young Ukrainian at the end of the 1920s and the beginning of the 1930s, who is trying to find a place for Ukraine in the world and for her cultural and national development.'[9] Samchuk's other novels were *Kulak* (The Fist, 1932), *Maria* (1934), and *Hory hovoriat* (The Mountains Are Speaking, 1934). His career as a novelist continued less successfully after 1946.

Leonid Mosendz (1897–1948) was a chemist by profession and lived in Czechoslovakia. He was a minor poet, author of the collection *Zodiak* (1941), and also wrote a short novel, *Zasiv* (Sowing, 1936). His major novel appeared later (see page 99).

In the 1920s an erstwhile modernist poet, Bohdan Lepky, became a successful novelist. His finest novel, *Pid tykhy vechir* (On a Quiet Evening), appeared in 1923, 'wrapped in a web of Indian summer and melancholy.'[10] More popular was Lepky's tetralogy *Mazepa* – composed of *Motria* (1926), *Ne vbyvai* (Do Not Kill, 1926), *Baturyn* (1927), and *Poltava* (1928) – which idealized the great hetman. Notwithstanding his nationalist interpretation, Lepky's name was restored to the literary world in 1988, when some of his early poetry was republished.

Other historical novelists published in Galicia during this period were Andrii Chaikovsky (1857–1935), Osyp Nazaruk (1883–1940), and Iuliian Opilsky (1884–1937). Especially noteworthy are Nazaruk's novels *Roksoliana* (1930) and *Iaroslav Osmomysl* (1920), and Opilsky's *Idu na vas* (I March against You, 1918). Another historical novelist, Katria Hrynevycheva (1875–1947), was the author of *Sholomy v sontsi* (Helmets under the Sun, 1929). The prose writer Halyna Zhurba (1888–1979) began her literary career in the pre-revolutionary journal *Ukrainska khata*. She wrote the novels *Zori svit zapovidaiut* (Stars Announce a Dawn, 1933) and *Revoliutsiia ide* (A Revolution Is Coming, 1937), and in 1975 her engaging autobiography was published.

To sum up, one can say that in the period between the wars Ukrainian writers west of the river Zbruch were less productive but more fortunate than those in the Soviet Ukraine. The region produced one truly major poet, Antonych, but lagged behind Soviet Ukraine in innovative prose. The stamp of emigration, with its nostalgia for and idealization of Ukraine, was a characteristic of the work of many writers in Prague and Warsaw, overshadowing whatever contacts they might have had with Central and Western Europe – for they kept in touch with Paris, Berlin, and Rome, not to mention Vienna. Most Western Ukrainian writers, with the exception of Sovietophiles, were nationalist and anti-Communist in their ideology. There were frequent crossings of swords with their Soviet counterparts: Malaniuk versus Sosiura, Dontsov, and Khvylovy. The future of 'greater Ukraine' moved their feelings more than anything else and often outweighed artistic considerations. It all came to an abrupt end in 1939, with the incorporation of Western Ukraine into the U.S.S.R. Only the émigré writers, now strengthened by the influx of new refugees from Soviet occupation, defiantly continued their isolation from their native land.

7 The Second Emigration and Diaspora 1945–90

The Second World War brought untold suffering to the Ukrainian people. Their territory and population were savaged by both the Wehrmacht and the Red Army. Politically and militarily Ukrainian resistance to German and Russian occupation showed itself in partisan warfare (UPA). Throughout the hostilities literature remained silent about the war-torn territories. An exception was some insignificant insurgent poetry.

In 1945 a group of Ukrainian refugee writers formed an organization called Mystetsky ukrainsky rukh, the Ukrainian Artistic Movement (MUR), in Fürth, Germany. It was headed by Ulas Samchuk, with Iurii Sherekh (the pseudonym of George Y. Shevelov) as his deputy. The organization held three conventions and published three MUR collections. According to the chief ideologist of MUR, Iurii Sherekh, 'the initiators of MUR thought that the path to world recognition lay solely in the unique, organic, and inimitable originality of Ukrainian literature. Hence came its declaration "to serve, in an accomplished form, its people and thereby win authority in world art." '[1]

At the same time, members of MUR tried to steer clear of émigré politics. Their concept of a national literature with its own style has been sharply attacked recently by G. Grabowicz.[2] Yet it is possible to point to the solid literary achievements of MUR in the short period of 1945–9. In prose, Iurii Kosach contributed a historical novel, *Den hnivu* (The Day of Anger, 1948); Dokiia Humenna (b. 1904) wrote a trilogy, *Dity chumatskoho shliakhu* (Children of the Chumak Pathway, 1948–51); Leonid Lyman (b. 1922) published excerpts from a novel, *Povist pro Kharkiv* (A Tale about Kharkiv, English translation, 1958); Ivan Bahriany

(1907–63) offered a successful novel of adventure, *Tyhrolovy* (The Hunters and the Hunted, 1946; English translation, 1954); Viktor Domontovych (1894–1969) produced a long story, *Doktor Serafikus* (1947), as well as a superb modernistic novel, *Bez gruntu* (Rootless, 1948); and Ulas Samchuk published the autobiographical novel *Iunist Vasylia Sheremety* (The Youth of Vasyl Sheremeta, 1946–7). Samchuk's novel about the great famine, *Temnota* (Darkness, 1957), was published in the United States. In the field of drama, *Diistvo pro Iuriia peremozhtsia* (A Play about Iurii the Conqueror, 1947) by Kosach and *Blyzniata shche zustrinutsia* (The Twins Will Meet Again, 1948) and *Diistvo pro velyku Liudynu* (A Play about a Great Man, 1948) by Kostetsky (1913–83) should be mentioned. Kostetsky's plays are very innovative.

The DP (Displaced Persons) poets were especially active. Older ex-Soviet poets wrote some fine works: for example, *Poet* (The Poet, 1947) by Todos Osmachka and *Popil imperii* (Ashes of the Empires, 1946) by Iurii Klen (pseudonym of Osvald Burkhardt). Klen also wrote a short book of memoirs, *Spohady pro neoklasykiv* (Memories of the Neoclassicists, 1947). A major new poet, Vasyl Barka (b. 1908), emerged among the refugees from Eastern Ukraine. As a DP he published two collections of poems: *Apostoly* (The Apostles, 1946) and *Bily svit* (A White World, 1947). 'Barka's *Weltanschauung* is based on two traditions: an ascetic, Slavic, and beneficent, biblical religion on the one hand, and a sensual love for the colourful riches of life, perhaps originating in folklore, on the other.'[3]

Another newcomer, the brother of Mykola Zerov, was Mykhailo Orest (1901–63), author of the collection of poems *Dusha i dolia* (Soul and Fate, 1946). Ivan Bahriany published the collection of poems *Zoloty bumerang* (The Golden Boomerang, 1946) and Bohdan Nyzhankivsky (1909–86) the collection *Shchedrist* (Generosity, 1947). Ostap Tarnavsky (b. 1917) produced *Slova i mrii* (Words and Dreams, 1948), Ihor Kachurovsky (b. 1918) wrote the collection *Nad svitlym dzherelom* (On the Bright Water Well, 1948) and Iar Slavutych (b. 1918) wrote *Homin vikiv* (The Echo of Centuries, 1946). Oleh Zuievsky (b. 1920) was the author of *Zoloti vorota* (The Golden Gate, 1947) Mykhailo Sytnyk (1920–59) of *Vidlitaiut ptytsi* (The Birds Are Flying Off, 1946), and Leonid Poltava of *Zhovti karuseli* (Yellow Carousels, 1948). Bohdan Kravtsiv's selected poems were entitled *Korabli* (Ships, 1948).

By 1949 MUR had stopped functioning. A new emigration, beyond the Atlantic, awaited most of the DP writers. They must, therefore, be judged as émigrés who preserved some of the best traditions of Ukrainian literature and often looked back rather than ahead.

Before we leave the European scene and follow the émigrés to the United States and Canada, where most of them were destined to live, it is necessary to glance at that part of the Ukrainian territory that had remained outside the Soviet Ukraine – the Presov region of Eastern Slovakia. After 1945 this area underwent gradual Ukrainization, leaving behind both Russian and Rusyn literary and linguistic influences. In 1951, by Party decree, Ukrainian was introduced into Transcarpathian schools in Slovakia as the language of instruction. About the same time new literary magazines were founded, among them *Duklia* (a quarterly after 1953, a bimonthly after 1966). Literary life was enlivened by the so-called Prague Spring (1968), when the literary movement was led by a talented critic and scholar, Orest Zilynsky (1923-76). After the Soviet invasion in 1968 this momentum was lost.

Several poets in Transcarpathia deserve to be mentioned. Vasyl Grendzha-Donsky (1897-1974) started writing poetry in the 1920s. Among his very traditional collections are *Shliakhom ternovym* (Along a Thorny Path, 1924, 1964) and *Misiachni hruni* (The Moon's Hills, 1969). He also wrote plays and novels. Fedir Lazoryk (b. 1913) was the author of *Slovo hnanykh i holodnykh* (The Word of the Hungry and Persecuted, 1949) and *Snizhni khryzantemy* (Snowy Chrysanthemums, 1968). Ivan Matsynsky (1922-87), whose first work had been in Russian, published *Prystritnyky* (Encounters, 1968). Iurii Bacha (b. 1932) was imprisoned following the invasion of 1968. The most prominent poet of the younger generation was Stepan Hostyniak (b. 1941), the author of *Proponuiu vam svoiu dorohu* (I Propose My Way to You, 1965), *Lyshe dvoma ochyma* (Only with Two Eyes, 1967), *Buket* (Bouquet, 1979), and *Anatomiia druhoho oblychchia* (An Anatomy of the Other Face, 1987).

Among the prominent Transcarpathian prose writers were Vasyl Zozuliak (b. 1909), the author of the epic trilogy *Neskoreni* (Unconquered, 1962-73), Mykhailo Shmaida (b. 1920), the author of *Trishchat kryhy* (The Ice Is Breaking, 1958), and Ieva Biss (b. 1921), whose short stories were collected in *Sto sim modnykh zachisok* (One Hundred and Seven Modern Hairdos, 1967) and *Apartment z viknom na holovnu vulytsiu* (Apartment with a Window Facing Main Street, 1969). Orest Zilynsky commented on her work:

Nevertheless this is prose in which the central place is occupied not by the story line, not by the narration of events, but by the creative discovery of the inner world of the protagonists ... There is an interest in the social topic, a meaningful, well-developed story, and a desire to unravel the wider contexts of reality. Firstly, she enlarges the thematic sphere, successfully showing the life of the pre- and post-war intelligentsia; secondly, she gives this a new psychological dimension, raising the human images to a common denominator of important moral ideas.[4]

Other prose writers from Transcarpathia were Vasyl Datsei (b. 1936) and Iosyf Shelepets (b. 1938). No outstanding playwrights came from that region.

The shores of the New World proved hospitable to the second wave of émigré writers. They dispersed across the North American continent and settled in cities, chiefly New York, Philadelphia, Chicago, Detroit, Montreal, Toronto, and Winnipeg. Although they eked out a modest existence (they were used to that), they found the time to write and to publish. They clung to familiar themes and continued their writing careers undisturbed. Some were past their prime, but others achieved a new fulfilment.

The doyen of émigré poets, Ievhen Malaniuk, published several collections of poetry – *Vlada* (Power, 1951), *Ostannia vesna* (The Last Spring, 1959), and *Serpen* (August, 1964) – as well as two volumes of incisive essays, *Knyha sposterezhen* (A Book of Observations, 1962–6). In his poems the old apocalyptic vision of Ukraine remained unaltered. His pamphlets on Little-Russianism, Bolshevism, and Mazepa are full of stimulating ideas.

Bohdan Kravtsiv published two collections of verse with untranslatable titles in the United States: *Zymozelen* (1951) and *Dzvenyslava* (1962). His collected works in two volumes appeared in New York in 1968–70. The poems of the prolific Vasyl Barka appeared in several collections: *Psalom holubynoho polia* (The Psalm of the Dove Field, 1958), *Okean* (The Ocean, 1959), and *Lirnyk* (The Lyre Player, 1968). He also wrote prose in *Rai* (Paradise, 1953) and *Zhovty kniaz* (The Yellow Prince, 1963). A monumental four-volume cycle of poems, *Svidok* (Witness), was published in 1981.

Todos Osmachka wrote a novel about the collectivization of agriculture, *Plan do dvoru* (A Plan for the Court, 1951), and a collection of short stories, *Rotonda dushohubtsiv* (A Rotunda of Murderers, 1956). He also translated Shakespeare and Oscar Wilde. Leonid Mosendz's greatest work, his novel dealing with Hebrew history, *Ostannii prorok* (The Last Prophet, 1960), was published posthumously.

Ivan Bahriany, who remained in Western Europe, published in 1950 a novel about a Soviet prison, *Sad hetsymansky* (The Orchard of Gethsemane, republished in Ukraine in 1990), and in 1957 a historical novel, *Marusia Bohuslavka*. Ihor Kachurovsky, who also stayed in Europe, wrote some excellent prose: *Shliakh nevidomoho* (The Path of the Unknown One, 1956), *Dim and krucheiu* (The House on the Cliff, 1966), as well as some translations.

Oleh Zuievsky, who emigrated to the United States and later to Canada, issued the collection of poems *Pid znakom Feniksa* (Under the Sign of the Phoenix, 1958). He is a translator of Emily Dickinson, Rilke, Mallarmé, and Stefan George. Iar Slavutych published his collected poems *Trofei* (Trophies, 1963) in Canada. He also translated Keats. Oleksa Veretenchenko (b. 1918) wrote two collections of poems: *Dym vichnosti* (The Eternal Fire, 1951) and *Chorna dolyna* (Black Valley, 1953). Natalia Livytska-Kholodna went to the United States, where she published a volume of late poems, *Poezii stari i novi* (Poems Old and New, 1986), which drew praise from George Shevelov.

Iurii Kosach, living in New York, joined a Sovietophile circle. He continued to publish some good prose, such as the historical novels, *Volodarka Pontydy* (Regina Pontica, 1987), *Suziriia lebedia* (The Constellation of the Swan, 1983), and *Chortivska skelia* (The Devil's Rock, 1988). Another prose writer, Ulas Samchuk, published a book of war memoirs, *Piat po dvanadtsiatii* (Five Past Twelve, 1954), and two somewhat less successful novels, *Na tverdii zemli* (On Solid Land, 1968) and *Choho ne hoit vohon* (What Fire Doesn't Heal, 1959). The old émigrés were showing some signs of exhaustion. Most valuable, however, were the collected editions of such writers as Klen, Kravtsiv, and Liaturynska, which were published posthumously in the United States and Canada.

A new generation of poets, born in Europe in the late 1920s and 1930s but hardly classifiable as émigrés, came to the fore in the United States in the late 1950s and the 1960s. Their works differed radically in style and structure from those of their predecessors. Their experience was of the New World, with only an occasional echo of the homeland.

Some of them formed the so-called New York Group of Poets and published their works under that group's auspices as well as in the journal *Novi poezii* (New Poems). Among the founders of the group, which had no organizational structure, were Emma Andievska, Bohdan Boichuk, Patricia Kilina, Bohdan Rubchak, Iurii Tarnavsky, Zhenia Vasylkivska, and Vira Vovk. They were united 'by a common desire for renewal in literary expression. All the members of the New York Group had their own individual interests and each created in his own way, without any obligation to adhere to a program.'[5] The innovation that the group brought to Ukrainian literature was not only linguistic but ideological. They downgraded provincialism and opened up new vistas to the outside world.

The most avant-garde writer in the New York Group, who later lived in West Germany, was Emma Andievska (b. 1931). Her first poems were greeted with both great approval and severe disapproval. Her publications are *Narodzhennia idola* (Birth of an Idol, 1958), *Ryba i rozmir* (Fish and Measurement, 1961), *Pervni* (Elements, 1964), *Bazar* (Market-Place, 1967), *Pisni bez tekstu* (Songs without Text, 1968), *Nauka pro zemliu* (Earth Sciences, 1975), and *Vigilii* (Vigils, 1987). An early critic noted that 'Andievska has created a world of her own ... a world that is rarely beautiful and moving. As with children's painting one can apply to her Tsvetaeva's words about Pasternak: a complete opening – only an opening into a different world and under a different sky than Pasternak ... The world and the sky reveal themselves to Andievska as unique; her poetry is international or, if you will, universal.'[6] Andievska's great originality in the use of language and poetic structure is not limited to her poetry. Her novels, notably *Herostraty* (Herostratoses, 1971), *Roman pro dobru liudynu* (A Novel about a Good Person, 1973), and *Roman pro liudske pryznachennia* (A Novel about Human Destiny, 1982), have won critical acclaim.

Zhenia Vasylkivska (b. 1929) published a single collection of verse, *Korotki viddali* (Short Distances, 1959). Patricia Kilina (b. 1936), of non-Ukrainian origin, learned the language well enough to write three collections of verse: *Trahediia dzhmeliv* (Tragedy of the Bumblebees, 1960), *Lehendy i sny* (Legends and Dreams, 1964), and *Rozhevi mista* (Pink Cities, 1969). Her philosophical poetry is very different from that of Vira Vovk (b. 1926), a professional linguist and professor of literature in Rio de Janeiro. Vovk's collections include *Chorni akatsii* (Black Acacias, 1961), *Liubovni lysty kniazhny Veroniky do kardynala Dzhovanni-patisty* (Love Letters of Princess Veronica to Cardinal Giovanni Battista, 1967), and *Kappa Khresta* (Kappa Crucis, 1969). She has also written Ukrainian and Portuguese poems in *Mandala* (1980), *Tryptykh* (Priptico, 1982), and *Sviaty hai* (Bosque Sagrado, 1983), and the prose works *Dukhy i dervishi* (Ghosts and Dervishes, 1956) and *Vitrazhi* (Vitraux, 1961). Vovk is a very prolific writer and translator. In many of her works – for example, *Ikonostas Ukrainy* (The Iconostasis of Ukraine, 1988) – she shows her abiding interest in her native land.

The leading poets among the men of the group were Bohdan Boichuk, Bohdan Rubchak, and Iurii Tarnavsky. Boichuk (b. 1927) is the author of *Chas boliu* (A Time of Pain, 1957), *Spomyny liubovy* (Memories of Love, 1963), *Virshi dlia Mekhiko* (Verses for Mexico, 1964), *Mandrivka til* (Journey of Bodies, 1967), *Virshi vybrani i peredostanni* (Poems Selected and Next to Last, 1983), and a long poem *Podorozh z uchytelem* (Journey with a Teacher, 1976). His plays *Dvi dramy* (Two Dramas, 1968) consist of *Holod–1933* (Famine–1933) and *Pryrecheni* (Doomed). A selection of his poetry in English translation, *Memories of Love*, was published in 1989.

An original talent in poetry was shown by Bohdan Rubchak (b. 1935), whose collections are *Promenysta zrada* (Bright Betrayal, 1960), *Divchyni bez krainy* (To a Girl without a Country, 1963), *Osobysta Klio* (A Personal Clio, 1967), and *Krylo Ikarove* (The Wing of Icarus, 1983). In 1989 a Soviet Ukrainian magazine published a selection of Rubchak's poetry, with the following appreciation, stressing the poet's 'ability to preserve his spiritual core, his roots among many cultural influences ... The hero of Rubchak's poetry is a man of contemporary urban culture, in a world of a hundred mirrors, the "dove-coloured sky" of the street, not the "blue sky of the spring," full of nostalgia, capable of resurrecting "the miracle of forgotten deities," to enliven the old roots of Slavic mythology, the indestructible elements of family and people.'[7]

Iruii Tarnavsky (b. 1934), a scientist by profession, is the author of *Zhyttia v misti* (Life in a City, 1956), *Popoludni v Pokipsi* (Afternoon in Poughkeepsie, 1960), *Idealizovana biografiia* (An Idealized Biography, 1964), *Bez Espanii* (Without Spain, 1969), and the short novel *Shliakhy* (Pathways, 1961). 'Of the entire New York Group Iurii Tarnavsky has, perhaps, the fewest forerunners, especially in Ukrainian or general Slavic literature. Ukrainians have in him not only a very talented poet, but also an envoy to the modern congress of poets, who often create in two languages and consciously reject any peculiarities determined by their national roots.'[8] In 1970 Tarnavsky published his collected poems in one volume, *Poezii pro nishcho i inshi poezii na tsiu samu temu* (Poems about Nothing and Other Poems on the Same Subject). His English novel *Meningitis* appeared in 1978.

Outside of the New York Group the following contemporary poets deserve to be mentioned: Marta Kalytovska (1916–90), Iurii Kolomyiets (b. 1930), Lida Palii (b. 1926), Leonid Poltava (b. 1921) and Oleh Zuievsky.

The least developed literature in the diaspora is in Australia, where an older prose writer, Dmytro Nytchenko (pseudonym Chub, b. 1905) and the satirical poet Zoia Kohut (b. 1925) have published their work.

The post-modernist era has not yet produced any outstanding writers in the diaspora. A host of young men and women continue to write and publish quasi-modernist poems, some in English but most in Ukrainian. In the latest wave of Ukrainian writers in the diaspora the following have made a name for themselves: Roman Baboval (b. 1950 in Belgium), the author of *Podorozh poza formy* (Travel beyond Forms, 1972) and *Nichni perekazy* (Evening Legends, 1987); Maria Revakovych (b. 1960 in Poland, now in the United States), the author of *Z mishka mandrivnyka* (From a Traveller's Bag, 1987) and *Shepotinnia, shepotinnia* (Whispering, Whispering, 1989); Mykhailo Mykhailuk (b. 1940 in Romania), author of the novel *Ne vir kryku nichnoho ptakha* (Don't Trust the Call of the Night Bird, 1981); Ivan Kovach (b. 1946 in Romania), author of *Zhyttia bez komy* (Life without a Coma, 1986); Mykola Korsiuk (b. 1950 in Romania), author of a collection of short stories, *Chuzhy bil* (Alien Pain, 1985); Tadei Karabovych (b. 1959 in Poland), author of *Volohist zemli* (Dampness of the Soil, 1986); and Iurii Havryliuk (b. 1964 in Poland), author of *Neherbovii genealohii* (Genealogies without a Crest, 1988). A special place in the diaspora is held by a Soviet Ukrainian immigrant to Germany, Moisei Fishbein (b. 1946), author of *Zbirka bez nazvy* (Without a Title, 1984). So far, nothing truly outstanding has been written in Australia. In Canada several published authors of Ukrainian descent – among them Myrna Kostash, Ted Galay, and Andrew Suknaski – are writing in English.

The existence of the New York Group purified Ukrainian literature. Questions have been raised about parallel literary developments in

Ukraine and the diaspora. There are few similarities except for the general striving here and there to rediscover the function of poetry. Since 1988 many poets in the diaspora have been published in Ukraine. This is more than a symbolic gesture of cultural unity. It is an acknowledgment of the end of the enforced isolation of Soviet Ukrainian literature and its readmission to a European home. Despite further political uncertainties the future of Ukrainian literature seems at the moment assured.

8 The Era of *Glasnost* 1987–90

The latest literary developments must, once more, be seen in the light of the political events that have recently transformed Eastern Europe and the Soviet Union. The engineer of these changes was Mikhail Gorbachev, who came to power in 1985. Two years later, in announcing his plan of *perestroika*, restructuring, and *glasnost*, openness, he declared: 'I agree that there should be no forgotten names or blank spots in either history or literature. Otherwise, what we have is not history or literature but artificial, opportunistic constructs.'[1] This quotation was seized upon in Ukraine and indeed in the entire Soviet Union by those who wanted to restore the 'forgotten names' and fill the 'blank spots' in literature. Gradually it has led to the widespread, almost complete rehabilitation of those writers who perished in the 1930s. In Ukraine it has meant the restoration of hundreds of names, this time including Mykola Khvylovy, Valeriian Pidmohylny, Mykhailo Semenko, and many others who were still banned in the 1960s. So far, the only writer beyond the pale of rehabilitation is Arkadii Liubchenko. The destruction of the Ukrainian intelligentsia in the 1930s has come to be viewed as similar in nature to the destruction of the Ukrainian peasantry in the man-made famine of 1932–3 in which seven million peasants were said to have perished.

One of the questions that has been raised is just how many writers actually were destroyed. Unexpected help in estimating the losses has come from a Russian source. In 1988 a Russian researcher, Eduard Beltov, published the results of his study of the purges of all Soviet writers. Of these, 'almost 500' came from Ukraine (see page 55). Beltov's staggering figure may be a little inflated. My own research showed 254

writers as victims of the purges. Later, in 1989, Mykola Zhulynsky gave
the total approximate figure as 300.[2] In 1991 *Literaturna Ukraina* began
publishing weekly listings and short biographies of the victims of
repression. The grim task continues. It will be followed by the republication of the banned works, if the supply of paper allows it.

Among the many republished or newly discovered works, some have
particular human and intellectual rather than artistic interest. In this
category are Sosiura's reminiscences, Khvylovy's article 'Ukraina chy
Malorosiia' (Ukraine or Little Russia), Hryhorii Kochur's publication of
some early poems by Tychyna, and letters from the Gulag by Zerov
and Pidmohylny. Very little of value has come from the meagre literature 'for the drawer' (written but unpublished under Stalin and
Brezhnev). The state of cultural deprivation is greater today in Ukraine
than in Eastern Europe. True, some memory and reverence for the
European high culture has survived, ironically enough, just when this
high culture is under attack in the free societies of the West.

At the end of 1987 an important conference was convened by the
Academy of Sciences in Kiev and the Ukrainian Writers' Union, setting
out guidelines for the restoration of the literature of the 1920s and 1930s.[3]

The rehabilitation of writers has spread to the pre-Soviet period. Not
only have the prominent writers of the nineteenth century – for example, Panteleimon Kulish and Borys Hrinchenko – been republished,
but the Ukrainian modernists of the twentieth century, such as Oles
and Vorony, have been returned to their readers as well. Literary scholars and critics have begun to rewrite the history of Ukrainian literature
from a non-Soviet point of view. This is not always easy, but genuine
attempts are being made at an objective evaluation. A history of
Ukrainian literature in two volumes, published in 1988, was severely
criticized for its old stereotypes. The first volume of the *Ukrainian
Literary Encyclopaedia* (1988) contained many entries for writers hitherto
banned – for example Vynnychenko – as well as information on such
émigré writers as Bahriany, Boichuk, and Vovk. These are all good
signs of a determined drive to re-evaluate the literature of the past.

The years 1989 and 1990 saw intense political activity in Ukraine, in
which many writers were involved. Ivan Drach, Dmytro Pavlychko,
and Volodymyr Iavorivsky came to head the National Movement for
Restructuring, known as Rukh, an umbrella organization of reform-
minded and democratic individuals. The Ukrainian Helsinki Group,

no longer underground, was part of it. Rukh adopted an openly nationalist platform, espousing full Ukrainian sovereignty. In cultural
matters it pleaded for the restoration of the Ukrainian heritage and for
independence from Moscow. In some ways Rukh's orientation was
similar to that of VAPLITE; a leader of Rukh, Drach, admitted that he
was following in the footsteps of Mykola Khvylovy.[4] The fact that the
political leadership of the reform movement was largely in the hands
of writers bears a striking resemblance to the situation in 1917.

   The new atmosphere of openness and free discussion has been very
stimulating for the flow of new ideas, but less so for creative writing.
Many authors, busy with politics, have no time or desire to write. There
is, therefore, at present a hiatus in literary creativity, which especially
affects the older writers. Ukraine has never lacked poets, however, and
some of the younger ones are full of promise. A new label – *visim-
desiatnyky* – has been attached to them, and they all seem to share a
bent towards the personal lyric. Without attempting to evaluate them,
I list the following: Iurii Andrukhovych (b. 1960), Natalka Bilotserkivets
(b. 1954), Pavlo Hirnyk (b. 1956), Oleksander Hrytsenko (b. 1957), Viktor
Kordun (b. 1946), Oleh Lysheha (b. 1949), Viktor Neborak (b. 1961),
Oksana Pakhlovska (b. 1956), Mykola Riabchuk (b. 1953), Volodymyr
Tsybulko (b. 1964), Oksana Zabuzhko (b. 1960) and, above all, Ihor
Rymaruk (b. 1958). Bohdan Rubchak, a perceptive critic, comments:

The younger poets of our time present a tremendous variety of styles, tech-
niques, and thematic fields. One may even say that such variety is almost too
dizzying. This is especially evident in the various critical texts – manifestoes
of sorts – where one direction seems to replace another almost as quickly as
literary theories replace each other in the West. The young poet Natalka Bilotserkivets, for example, assures us that the young poets who made their debuts
in the mid 1980s are now hopelessly antiquated, to be presently replaced by a
'new wave.'[5]

Rubchak distinguishes the 'philological' poets as well as the creators
of the 'poetry of statement,' and ends with this observation: 'It would
hardly be an exaggeration to say that dozens of poems published in
periodicals last year were devoted to the danger in which the Ukrainian
language finds itself today. We have also seen strong passages, or entire

poems, devoted to the hymning of the language as such. The language of poetry, in particular, is glorified as the only salvation in our world – the only love that will never betray.'[6]

The following are the best recent collections of poetry: *Ikar na metelykovykh krylakh* (Icarus on the Wings of a Butterfly, 1990) by Vasyl Holoborodko, *Pohulianka odyntsem* (Walking Alone, 1900) by Mykola Vorobiov, *Zemlia* (Earth, 1989) by Gennadii Moroz, *Dyrygenty ostannoi svichky* (The Holders of the Last Candle, 1990) by Oksana Zabuzhko, and *Khymera* (Chimera, 1989) by Vasyl Ruban. The poets Oleh Lysheha and Iurii Andrukhovych also write prose, and together with Ievhen Pashkovsky and Volodymyr Dibrova show a great deal of promise. According to a critic, 'the unexpected appearance of new and maturing prose is a most interesting phenomenon, completely new in its artistic thought and view of the world.'[7]

Of great benefit to Ukrainian literature was the recent publication in Ukraine of some émigré writers, hitherto denounced as 'bourgeois nationalists.' Among them were Iurii Klen, Ievhen Malaniuk, Oleh Olzhych, Olena Teliha, and many others. Many writers living and writing in the diaspora also appeared in print in Ukraine. The artificial 'iron curtain' for decades dividing the homeland and the emigration has been torn down. Some Ukrainian American scholars have appeared in print in Soviet Ukrainian journals. Many Ukrainian writers have visited the United States and Canada. The Ukrainian chapter of PEN International includes both Soviet Ukrainian and émigré writers.

Looking back at almost a century of Ukrainian literature, one is struck by the great changes, reflecting the political upheavals in the country. Unprotected by any national laws, constantly harassed by the police, with a readership intimidated by the country's oppressors, the writers fought a defensive battle for survival. At times, during the Stalin era, it seemed that even survival was uncertain. The role that literature assumed, as it did in the nineteenth century, of protecting human and national rights, drew it away from artistic pursuits. Yet the modernists' call to serve 'pure beauty' was never abandoned. There were always some writers who tried to follow that path. Many, however, were forced to write programmatic works that now seem valueless. The corruption of some of the most talented writers who had to serve the Communist Party is sad testimony not so much to human frailty as to the effectiveness of terror. There is ample evidence that while some were subdued but not conquered, many prostituted their art in the service of an ideology. The ravages of this moral decay will not disappear quickly.

Understandably writers, once freed from political controls, will turn to the neglected topics of recent history with all its traumas. Already this trend is in evidence, with many recent prose works and poems dedicated to the famine of 1932–3. There is, indeed, a whole host of themes, hitherto forbidden, which may now be appealing. There may, however, be a disenchantment with politics and history altogether, and this may provide a stimulus for the exploration of the self or for ecological concerns, which, after Chernobyl, are uppermost in many minds. In either case, the new literature may also be fantastic or surrealist rather than plainly realistic.

The recent climate of renewal has revived hopes for the free development of literature. This is what most writers in this century either secretly or openly desired. However, freedom imposes responsibilities that many are unable or unwilling to undertake. The organizational structure of the Writers' Union calls for radical reform, if not for outright abolition. Yet precisely now, when the need to organize politically is very great, there is a reluctance to step out of this Stalinist structure. Only the future will tell if a return to an earlier and happier time, when there were many groups and circles of writers, is possible. The heritage of command and monopoly is hard to shake off. Literary bureaucrats are still alive and well today.

The recent links with the diaspora forecast an end to a long period of isolation. Not much has been said in these pages about those who, under difficult circumstances, have tried to keep in touch with foreign literatures: the translators. Some of them – for example, Hryhorii Kochur – are now viewed as having performed a heroic task. More translations from foreign literature are on the way; the journal *Vsesvit* (Universe) has been dedicated exclusively to translation. Zerov's and Khvylovy's calls for a pro-Western orientation are no longer despised. The heritage of the émigré writers from Western Europe is now cherished and acknowledged.

In the perceptive words of the Australian critic, Marko Pavlyshyn, a real change in cultural attitudes is still far off.

The hagiographic quality of writing about literature, especially in encyclopaedia articles, biographical compendia and general histories, had been especially marked during High Stalinism and again in the 1970s. Literary history read like an account of the same ideologically sound person writing the same ideologically sound work over and over again. This, of course, has now changed. Not only are there new biographical motifs which, if invoked, signify favourable evaluation of a given writer by the critic or historian (books banned by the censorship, obstruction of publication, editorial mutilation, conflicts with officialdom and the KGB, even imprisonment), but the biographies themselves have become more factual, individualized, realistic and lively. The [literary] iconostasis, one might observe, is evolving from its Byzantine to its Baroque form. In particular, the central salvation narrative which the iconostasis illustrates is being modified: it no longer beckons toward the classless society, or the happy community of nations fused into one under the benign inspiration of the great Russian people ...

What happens to the new members of the iconostasis? They tend to be frozen into static poses, like everyone else. The rehabilitated from the 1920s and 1930s – Volodymyr Vynnychenko, Mykola Khvylovy, the neoclassicists Mykola Zerov, Mykhailo Drai-Khmara and Pavlo Fylypovych, the émigré Oleksander Oles, to name only the most prominent – are, for the moment at least, being treated as holy objects. Their names are honoured (often by inclusion in long lists of newly honourable names), their life stories are told, and the nature of their conflict with the Soviet state and its inevitable outcome are recorded. Often their works are published, either for the first time after a long hiatus, or in more complete and less expurgated editions. But there is little discussion of them as texts.[8]

Yet all this allows one, at the time of writing, to take a cautiously optimistic view of the present. The past is at last being re-evaluated without ideological strictures. Yet, ironically enough, the abolition of strictures has led to no blossoming but rather to the languishing of literature. The clear turn towards dictatorship in Gorbachev's policy during 1991, however, points to a danger of the re-imposition of controls over literature. At the moment, the democratization of the literary life and atmosphere, though undeniable, is still very fragile even after the declaration of independence in August 1991. Any reversal of *glasnost* could put a stop to it. One can only hope that this will not happen and that the end of the twentieth century may prove to be, as did the end of the nineteenth century, a fresh start in the neverending process of innovation in literature.

Notes

Chapter 1 Beginning a New Century

1 Franko, 'Z ostannikh desiatylit XIX v.,' *Zibrannia tvoriv* (Kiev 1984), vol. 41
2 Ibid., p. 250
3 Ibid., p. 523
4 I. Franko, 'Internatsionalizm i natsionalizm v suchasnykh literaturakh,' *Zibrannia tvoriv*, vol. 31
5 Ibid., p. 34
6 I. Franko, 'Iz sekretiv poetychnoi tvorchosty,' *Zibrannia tvoriv*, vol. 31
7 Ibid., p. 53
8 Ibid., p. 71
9 'Khronika: ukrainsky almanakh,' *Literaturno-naukovy vistnyk* (hereafter *LNV*) 16 (1901): 14
10 *LNV*, 6 (1903)
11 L. Ukrainka, *Tvory v dvanadsiaty tomakh* (Kiev 1979), vol. 12
12 Ibid., p. 29
13 Ibid., p. 51
14 K. Hryvenycheva, 'Nerozuminnia iako dokaz,' *LNV*, 6 (1903)
15 O.L., 'Moloda muza,' *Dilo*, 18 November 1907
16 All quotations are from O.L.[utsky]'s article, reprinted in *Ostap Lutsky – Molodomuzets* (Toronto 1968), 55–9
17 I. Franko, 'Manifest Molodoi Muzy,' *Dilo*, 13 December 1907
18 Ibid.
19 I. Franko, 'Pryvezeno zillia z triokh hir na vesillia, Moloda Muza 5,' *LNV* 40 (1907)
20 I. Franko, *Zibrannia tvoriv*, vol. 50, 331
21 M. Ievshan, *Pid praporom mystetstva* (Kiev 1910)

22 Ibid., 8

23 Ibid., 12

24 M. Sribliansky, 'Na suchasni temy,'*Ukrainska khata*, no. 2 (1911), 116

25 'Vid redaktsii,' *Ukrainska khata*, no. 1 (1909), 2

26 B. Rubchak, 'Probny let,' introduction to Iurii Lutsky, ed. *Ostap Lutsky – Molodomuzets* (Toronto 1968)

27 M. Kotsiubynsky, *Tvory v shesty tomakh* (Kiev 1961), vol. 5, 338

28 A. Krymsky, *Tvory v piaty tomakh* (Kiev 1972), vol. 1, 23

29 L. Ukrainka, *Tvory v dvanadtsiaty tomakh* (Kiev 1979), vol. 12, 137–50

30 O. Babyshkin, *Ahatanhel Krymsky* (Kiev 1967), 53–4

31 M. Stepniak, 'Poety Molodoi Muzy,' *Chervony shliakh*, no. 1 (1933)

32 I. Franko, *Zibrannia tvoriv*, vol. 33, 176

33 P. Karmansky, *Oi liuli smutku* (Lviv 1906), 5

34 O. Doroshkevych, *Pidruchnyk istorii ukrainskoi literatury* (Kharkiv 1927), 252

35 S. Cherkasenko, introduction to M. Vorony, *U siaivi mrii* (Kiev 1913), 6–9

36 O. Biletsky, 'Mykola Vorony,' *Zibrannia prats* (Kiev 1965), vol. 2, 612–14

37 P. Fylypovych, introduction to O. Oles, *Vybrani tvory* (Kiev 1925)

38 M. Zerov, *Do dzherel* (Kiev 1926), 75–6

39 M. Ievshan, 'Nash literaturny bilians za 1912 rik,' *LNV* 61 (1913): 167

40 M. Shapoval, 'Novyny nashoi literatury,' *LNV* 49 (1912): 626

41 M. Zhulynsky, 'Hryhorii Chuprynka,' *Literaturna Ukraina*, 28 July 1988

42 B. Iakubsky, 'Liryka Lesi Ukrainky,' *Tvory* (New York reprint 1953), vol. 2, xix

43 C. Bida, 'Life and Work,' *Lesia Ukrainka* (Toronto 1968), 46–7

44 M. Zerov, 'Lesia Ukrainka,' *Do dzherel* (Krakow-Lviv 1943) 176

45 L. Ukrainka, *Tvory*, vol. 12, 48

46 M. Ievshan, *Pid praporom mystetstva*, 79

47 P. Fylypovych, introduction to O. Kobylianska, *V nediliu rano zillia kopala* (Buenos Aires 1954), lv

48 I. Trush, 'Vasyl Stefanyk,' *Buduchnist*, 1 July 1899. Here reprinted from *Vasyl Stefanyk u krytytsi ta spohadakh* (Kiev 1970), 41

49 L. Ukrainka, 'Ukrainski pysmennyky na Bukovyni,' *Tvory*, vol. 8, 74

50 B. Rubchak, 'The Music of Satan and the Bedeviled World,' in M. Kotsiubynsky, *Shadows of Forgotten Ancestors* (Littleton 1981), 93–4

51 Ibid., 104

52 O. Stavytsky, 'Dramaturhiia,' *Istoriia ukrainskoi literatury v vosmy tomakh* (Kiev 1968), vol. 5, 471

53 O. Doroshkevych, *Pidruchnyk*, 231

54 L. Ukrainka, *Tvory*, vol. 11, 318

55 H. Khotkevych, 'Literaturni vrazhinnia,' *LNV* 43 (1908), 120
56 L. Kolakowski, 'Modernity on Endless Trial,' *Encounter*, March 1987, 10
57 See Iu. Shevelov, *Ukrainska mova v pershii polovyni dvadtsiatoho stolittia (1900–1941)* (New York 1987), 40–2
58 M. Rudnytsky, 'Ivan Franko,' in *Vid Myrnoho do Khvylovoho* (Lviv 1936), 169–70
59 Iu. Shevelov, 'Poza mezhi mozhlyvoho,' in Ivan Franko, *Moisei* (New York 1968), 118–19
60 M. Rudnytsky, *Vid Myrnoho do Khvylovoho*, 172
61 Ibid., 262
62 O. Zasenko, introduction to Osyp Makovei, *Vybrano tvory* (Kiev 1961), 23–4
63 M. Ievshan, 'Mykola Cherniavsky; proba kharakterystyky,' *LNV* 50 (1910), 253, 258
64 A. Nikovsky, 'Ukrainska literatura v 1912 r.' *LNV* 61 (1913), 170, 182

Chapter 2 The Failed Revolution

1 For details see my *Literary Politics in the Soviet Ukraine: 1917–34* (New York, 1956)
2 S. Iefremov, *Istoriia ukrainskoho pysmenstva* (Kiev-Leipzig 1924), vol. 2, 355–6
3 L. Novychenko, *Poeziia i revoliutsiia* (Kiev 1979)
4 V. Barka, *Khliborobsky orfei abo kliarnetyzm* (Munich, 1961)
5 O.S. Ilnytzkyj, 'Anatomy of a Literary Scandal: Myxajl Semenko and the Origins of Ukrainian Futurism,' *Harvard Ukrainian Studies*, December 1978, 478
6 Ibid., 497–9
7 O. Doroshkevych, *Pidruchnyk istorii ukrainskoi literatury* (Kharkiv 1927), 295
8 Ibid., 297–8
9 Iu. Sherekh (G.Y. Shevelov) 'Lehenda pro ukrainsky neokliassytsyzm' (written in 1944), *Ne dlia ditei* (New York 1964)
10 Ibid., 131
11 Ibid., 146–7
12 M. Tarnawsky, 'Valerijan Pidmohyl'nyj, Guy de Maupassant and the Magic of the Night,' unpublished PHD dissertation, Harvard University, 1986
13 Ibid., 311–12
14 M. Rylsky, 'Pro dvokh poetiv,' *Zhyttia i revoliutsiia*, no. 5 (1925), 85

15 I. Dziuba, 'Zasvityvsia sam od sebe,' *Literaturna Ukraina*, 22 October 1968

16 M. Ialovy, 'Pershi khorobri,' *Chervony shliakh*, no. 9 (1923), 115

17 V. Chumak, *Zaspiv*, here quoted from *Istoriia ukrainskoi literatury* (Kiev 1970), vol. 6, 105

18 M. Iohansen, 'Erotyzm v novii ukrainskii poezii,' *Zhovten* (1922), 98–9

19 V. Hadzinsky, introduction to H. Mykhailychenko, *Khudozhni tvory* (Kharkiv 1929), 69

20 Iu. Sherekh, *Ne dlia ditei*, 66

21 V. Iurynets, here quoted from A. Leites and M. Iashek, *Desiat rokiv ukrainskoi literatury (1917–27)* (Kharkiv 1928), vol. 1, 527

22 Iu. Sherekh, *Ne dlia ditei*, 55

23 M. Chyrkov, 'Mykola Khvylovy u ioho prozi,' *Zhyttia i revoliutsiia*, no. 10 (1925), 43

24 For a detailed discussion see M. Shkandrij, 'Literary Discussion in Soviet Ukraine, 1925–28,' unpublished PHD dissertation, University of Toronto, 1980

25 I.V. Stalin, *Sochineniia* (Moscow 1948), vol. 7, 153

26 Ia. Savchenko, 'Volodymyr Sosiura,' *Zhyttia i revoliutsiia*, no. 8 (1925), 19–20

27 V. Hryshko, ed., in V. Sosiura, *Zasudzhene i zaboronene* (New York 1952), 9

28 Iu. Lavrinenko, 'Mykola Bazhan,' *Rozstriliane vidrodzhennia* (Paris 1959), 307–8

29 E. Adelheim, *Mykola Bazhan* (Kiev 1974), 31

30 O. Biletsky, 'Pro prozu vzahali ta pro nashu prozu 1925 r.,' *Chervony shliakh*, no. 3 (1926), 155–6

31 O. Kylymnyk, *Iurii Ianovsky* (Kiev 1957), 61

32 O. Biletsky, 'Por prozu vzahali', 143

33 M. Khvylovy, here quoted from Leites and Iashek, vol. 1, 142

34 Ia. Savchenko, here quoted from Leites and Iashek, vol. 1, 447

35 M. Zhulynsky, 'Ivan Senchenko,' *Literaturna Ukraina*, 22 September 1988

36 O. Biletsky, 'Pro prozu vzahali,' 150

37 A. Leites, here quoted from Leites and Iashek, vol. 1, 195

38 A. Shamrai, ibid., 259–60

39 V. Skurativsky, 'Zamist pisliamovy,' *Prapor*, no. 9 (1990), 86

40 V. Zaets, 'Na chilnomu mistsi,' in *Pro Petra Pancha* (Kiev 1961), 70–1

41 O. Kylymnyk, 'Tvorchist Hryhoriia Epika,' in H. Epik, *Tvory* (Kiev 1958), 7–8

42 B. Shnaider, 'Oleksander Kopylenko,' in *Tvory* (Kiev 1961) vol. 1, 13

43 Iu. Sherekh, 'Kolir nestrymnykh palakhtin,' *Mur almanakh* (n.p. 1946), vol. 1, 156

44 Iu. Lavrinenko, 'Mykola Kulish,' *Rozstriliane vidrodzhennia*, 655–6

45 Iu. Sherekh, *Ne dlia ditei*, 81

46 N. Kuziakina, *Pesy Mykoly Kulisha* (Kiev 1970), 452

47 F. Iakubovsky, here quoted from Leites and Iashek, vol. 1, 247

48 B. Kovalenko, ibid., 75

49 Ia. Savchenko, ibid., 516

50 *Istoriia ukrainskoi literatury*, vol. 6, 191

51 Iu. Sherekh, 'Istroiia odniei literaturnoi mistyfikatsii,' in E. Strikha, *Parodezy, Zozendropia, Avtoekzekutsiia* (New York 1955), 255

52 S. Shakhovsky, 'Volodymyr Gzhytsky,' *Ukrainski radianski pysmennyky* (Kiev 1976), vol. 8, 176

53 Ibid., 171

54 A. Lebid, 'Od symvolizmu do revoliutsiinoi literatury,' *Zhyttia i revoliutsiia*, no. 6–7 (1925), 33

55 M. Dubyna, 'Neskorene slovo poeta,' in V. Bobynsky, *Poezii* (Kiev 1967), 13

56 Leites and Iashek, vol. 1, 193

57 O. Biletsky, 'Pro prozu vzahali,' 136

58 Ibid.

59 O. Kylymnyk, 'Z chystykh dzherel zhyttia,' in A. Holovko, *Tvory* (Kiev 1962), vol. 1, 6

60 Ibid., 21

61 I. Kapustianky, here quoted from Leites and Iashek, vol. 1, 387

62 Ibid., vol. 1, 370

63 O. Zasenko, 'Plomin zhyttia – ridnii literaturi,' in M. Tereshchenko, *Tvory* (Kiev 1968), vol. 1, 19

64 Iu. Kostiuk, 'Tvorchy shliakh Iakova Mamontova,' in Ia. Mamontov, *Tvory* (Kiev 1962), 18

65 N. Kuziakina, *Dramaturh Ivan Kocherha* (Kiev 1968), 62

66 Ibid., 97

67 M. Sýrotiuk, 'Slovo pro myttsia,' in I. Mykytenko, *Tvory* (Kiev 1964), vol. 1, xxiv

68 Quoted in *Istoriia ukrainskoi literatury*, vol. 6, 359

Chapter 3 The Trauma of Socialist Realism

1 Here quoted from *Istoriia ukrainskoi literatury* (Kiev 1971), vol. 7, 9

2 G. Luckyj, *Keeping a Record: Literary Purges in Soviet Ukraine (1930s), a Bio-Bibliography* (Edmonton 1987)

3 Interview with Eduard Beltov in *Knizhnoe obozrenie*, no. 25, (1988)

4 R. Conquest, *The Harvest of Sorrow* (New York, Oxford 1986)

5 A. Pohribny, 'Pro mimikriiu-pavliukiiu, zabuti imena abo bili pliamy,' *Literaturna Ukraina*, 15 September 1988

6 B. Oliinyk, 'Perebudovu slid pohlybliuvaty,' *Literaturna Ukraina*, 5 January 1989

7 Iu. Sherekh, *Ne dlia ditei* (New York 1964), 82

8 Quoted in G. Struve, *Russian Literature under Lenin and Stalin* (Norman, OK 1971), 262

9 G. Grabowicz, 'Tycyna's Cernihiv,' *Harvard Ukrainian Studies*, March 1977, 113

10 S. Shakhovsky, 'Pavlo Tychyna,' *Literaturni portrety* (Kiev 1960) vol. 1, 58

11 Iu. Lavrinenko, *Na shliakhakh syntezy kliarnetyzmu* (New York 1977)

12 S. Telniuk, 'Narodovi ie chym hordytysia,' *Literaturna Ukraina*, 6 October 1988

13 M. Rylsky, 'Mynaiut dni odnomanitni,' *Iskry vohniu velykoho* (Kiev 1965), 78

14 O. Biletsky, 'Tvorchist Maksyma Rylskoho,' in M. Rylsky, *Tvory v desiaty tomakh* (Kiev 1960), vol. 1, 21–2

15 Ibid., 25

16 Ie. Radchenko, *Volodymyr Sosiura* (Kiev 1967), 108

17 Ibid., 181

18 M. Bazhan, *Tvory v chotyriokh tomakh* (Kiev 1984), vol. 1, 119

19 Ibid., 24

20 Ibid., 179

21 M. Ostryk, in Iurii Ianovsky, *Opovidannia, romany, pesy* (Kiev 1984), 21

22 V. Donchyk, introduction to Petro Panch, *Povisti, opovidannia, humoresky, kazky* (Kiev 1985), 18

23 Ibid., 23

24 N. Kuziakina, *Dramaturh Ivan Korcherha* (Kiev 1968), 208

25 Quoted from *Pravda*, 24 December 1934, in I. Duz, *Oleksandr Korniichuk* (Kiev 1963), 46

26 Ibid., 70

27 O. Kudin, 'Leonid Pervomaisky,' *Literaturni portrety* (Kiev 1960), vol. 1, 544

28 V. Beliaev, 'Natan Rybak,' *Literaturni portrety*, vol. 2, 355

29 Ibid., 361

30 Ibid., 363

31 B. Buriak, 'Iakiv Kachura,' *Ukrainski radianski pysmennyky* (Kiev 1958), vol. 3, 228

32 H. Nudha, 'Teren Masenko,' *Tvory v dvokh tomakh* (Kiev 1963), 14

33 V. Ivanysenko, 'Dobrom nahrite sertse,' in A. Malyshko, *Tvory v piaty tomakh* (Kiev 1962), vol. 1, 8

34 Ibid., 20

34 Ibid., 20

35 V. Herasymchuk, 'V iakizh my ryby pidemo?' *Literaturna Ukraina*, 3 November 1988

36 I. Koshelivets, *Suchasna literatura v URSR* (New York 1964), 246

Chapter 4 The Thaw

1 M. Rylsky, 'Oleksandr Dovzhenko,' in O. Dovzhenko, *Tvory v triokh tomakh* (Kiev 1958), vol. 1, 6

2 I. Koshelivets, *Suchasna literatura v URSR* (New York 1964), 266–7

3 *Istoriia ukrainskoi literatury* (Kiev 1964), 808

4 M. Zhulynsky, 'Vasyl Symonenko,' *Literaturna Ukraina*, 24 March 1988

5 I. Drach, *Soniashnyk* (Kiev 1962), 13

6 B. Kravtsiv, *Shistdesiat poetiv shistdesiatykh rokiv* (New York 1967), v

7 Ibid.

8 M. Zhulynsky, *Nablyzhennia* (Kiev 1986), 93

9 Ibid., 95

10 V. Shevchuk, 'Demokratyzatsiia, hlasnist, literatura,' *Kyiv*, no. 11 (1988), 5

Chapter 5 From Stagnation to Reconstruction

1 P. Zahrebelny, 'Osiahnennia prostoty,' in P. Panch, *Tvory v shesty tomakh* (Kiev 1981), vol. 1, 12

2 V. Donchyk, *Iednist pravdy i prystrasti* (Kiev 1981), 129

3 A. Skrypnyk, 'Povertaiuchys do Vavilona,' *Literaturna Ukraina*, 13 October 1988

4 O. Honchar, 'A Portrayer of Truth,' in H. Tiutiunnyk, *Cool Mint* (Kiev 1986), 5

5 M. Slaboshpytsky, 'Z henetychnoi pamiati narodu,' *Literaturna Ukraina*, 26 January 1989

6 Interview in M. Zhulynsky, *Nablyzhennia* (Kiev 1986), 175

7 Ibid., 194

8 M. Pavlyshyn, 'Mythological, Religious, and Philosophical Topoi in the Prose of Valerii Shevchuk,' forthcoming in *Slavic Review*

9 M. Zhulynsky, *Nablyzhennia*, 228

10 Ibid., 206

11 V. Fashchenko, *Pavlo Zahrebelny* (Kiev 1984), 99
12 V. Fashchenko, 'Hlybin i rozmaittia dyvosvitu,' in P. Zahrebelny, *Tvory* (Kiev 1979), vol. 1, 11
13 M. Kundera, *The Art of the Novel* (New York 1986), 42
14 V. Donchyk, *Istyna-osobystist* (Kiev 1984), 185
15 Ibid., 191
16 M. Pavlyshyn, 'Ia Bohdan (spovid u slavi) Pavla Zahrebelnoho,' *Suchasnist*, no. 9 (1985), 35
17 M. Zhulynsky, *Nablyzhennia*, 153, 158
18 Ibid., 168
19 L. Fedorovska, *Romany Iuriia Mushketyka* (Kiev 1982), 170
20 V. Kachkan, *Roman Fedoriv* (Kiev 1983), 124
21 M. Zhulynsky, *Nablyzhennia*, 81
22 Ibid., 269
23 A. Makarov, 'Pisni pokhmurykh dniv,' *Literaturna Ukraina*, 19 May 1988
24 *Istoriia ukrainskoi literatury* (Kiev 1988), vol. 2, 669
25 G. Shevelov, 'Trunok i trutyzna,' in V. Stus, *Palimpsesty* (New York 1986), 21
26 B. Rubchak, 'Peremoha nad prirvoiu,' *Vasyl Stus* (Baltimore-Toronto 1987), 321
27 V. Swoboda, 'The Evolution of Mykola Rudenko's Philosophy in His Poetry,' *Studia Ucrainica*, no. 4 (1988), 83
28 I. Dziuba, 'Tsiliushcha sil samopiznannia,' in P. Movchan, *Sil* (Kiev 1989), 9

Chapter 6 Western Ukraine and Emigration

1 B. Rubchak, introduction to B. Antonych, *Square of Angels* (Ann Arbor, MI 1977), xix–xx
2 B. Boichuk and B. Rubchak, *Koordynaty* (New York 1969), vol. 1, 35–6
3 Ibid., 266–7
4 Ibid., 161
5 Ibid., 66
6 Iu. Shevelov, 'Nad kupkoiu popelu shcho bula Oksanoiu Liaturynskoiu,' in O. Liaturynska, *Zibrani tvory* (Toronto 1983), 63
7 *Koordynaty*, vol. 2, 302
8 Ibid., 88
9 B. Kravtsiv, 'Samchuk,' in V. Kubiovych, ed., *Entsyklopediia ukrainoznavstva* (Munich 1973), 2704

10 Ie. Pelensky, 'Bohdan Lepky – poet,' in *Bohdan Lepky* (Krakow-Lviv 1943), 21

Chapter 7 The Second Emigration and Diaspora

1 Iu. Sherekh, 'Ukrainska emihratsiina literatura v Evropi 1945–49,' *Ne dlia ditei* (New York 16964), 233
2 H. Hrabovych, 'Velyka literatura,' *Suchasnist*, no. 7–8 (1986)
3 B. Boichuk and B. Rubchak, *Koordynaty* (New York 1969), vol. 2, 62
4 O. Zilynsky, 'Na shliakhu do liudynoznavstva,' *Duklia*, no. 1 (1968), 55. Here quoted from S. Sirka, *The Development of Ukrainian Literature in Czechoslovakia, 1945–75* (Frankfurt 1978), 111–12
5 V. Vovk in an interview by I. Fizer, *Suchasnist*, no. 10 (1988), 16
6 E. Rais, 'Poeziia E. Andievskoi,' *Suchasnist*, no. 2 (1963), 51
7 B. Rubchak, 'Rozryv-trava,' *Zhovten*, no. 6 (1989), 6
8 *Koordynaty*, vol. 2, 387

Chapter 8 The Era of *Glasnost*

1 Here quoted from 'Gorbachev Sets Guidelines for Journalists,' *Current Digest of the Soviet Press*, vol. 39, no. 7 (18 March 1987), 7. For the original see M.S. Gorbachev, *Izbrannye rechi i stati* (Moscow 1987), vol. 4, 373
2 M. Zhulynsky, 'Iz falanhy vybuvaly naikrashchi,' *Suchasnist*, no. 10 (1989), 32
3 For details see G. Luckyj, *Literary Politics in the Soviet Ukraine, 1917–1934*, 2nd ed. (Durham 1990), 258–63
4 Ibid., 266
5 B. Rubchak, 'Because We Have No Time: New Poetry in 1988,' in R. Bahry, ed., *Echoes of Glasnost in Soviet Ukraine*, (Toronto 1990), 131
6 Ibid., 147
7 O. Zabuzhko, '1989-yi uviide v literaturu pid znakom nadii,' *Literaturna Ukraina* 26 April 1990
8 Marko Pavlyshyn, 'Aspects of the Literary Process in the USSR: The Politics of Re-Canonization in Ukraine After 1985,' forthcoming in *Southern Review* (Adelaide)

A Note on English Translations

Occasionally in the text mention is made of English translations of Ukrainian literary works. For a more complete source of translations consult the following recent publications: Oksana Piaseckyj, *Bibliography of Ukrainian Literature in English and French*, Ottawa 1989; Marta Tarnawsky, *Ukrainian Literature in English*, Edmonton 1989, and Bohdan S. Wynar, *Ukraine: A Bibliographic Guide to English-Language Publications*, Englewood, NJ, 1990.

Index of Authors and Titles

www.ingramcontent.com/pod-product-compliance
Ingram Content Group UK Ltd.
Pitfield, Milton Keynes, MK11 3LW, UK
UKHW020726050325
455857UK00007B/29